# The Faculty Lounges

# The Faculty Lounges

## and Other Reasons Why You Won't Get the College Education You Paid For

NAOMI SCHAEFER RILEY

IVAN R. DEE
*Chicago*

Published by Ivan R. Dee
A wholly owned subsidiary of The Rowman & Littlefield Publishing Group, Inc.
4501 Forbes Boulevard, Suite 200, Lanham, Maryland 20706
http://www.rowmanlittlefield.com

Estover Road, Plymouth PL6 7PY, United Kingdom

Distributed by National Book Network

www.ivanrdee.com

Library of Congress Cataloging-in-Publication Data
Riley, Naomi Schaefer.
  The faculty lounges : and other reasons why you won't get the college education you paid for / Naomi Schaefer Riley.
      p. cm.
  Includes index.
  ISBN 978-1-56663-886-9 (cloth : alk. paper) — ISBN 978-1-56663-888-3 (electronic)
  1. Education, Higher—United States. I. Title.
  LA227.4.R55 2011
  378.73—dc22                                                          2010051677

To Mom, Dad, Jason, Emily, and Simon

# Contents

# Preface

"First get tenure, then hoist the Jolly Roger." I learned that pearl of pragmatic wisdom, originally offered by the eminent Harvard political scientist Harvey Mansfield, from my father somewhere around the time I was in sixth grade. For my father, a political science professor at a small college in Massachusetts, as for Mansfield, the institution of tenure has allowed him the freedom to be a serious contrarian on his campus. Whether he was giving difficult exams in an era of grade inflation or asking critical questions about the politically correct ideas of the day, tenure meant that he didn't have to risk his family's livelihood to defend what he believed in. It protected him from capricious administrators and angry colleagues, and (in my biased opinion) it gave his students a deeper and more well-rounded education. For the record, I have no doubt that my father—who in his childhood was expelled from kindergarten for his defiance—would have spoken his mind either way. But tenure made his principled stance a little less dangerous.

In the academic world, my father was (and is) one of the "haves." He made it to a prestigious school in a city in the Northeast and has remained there for almost thirty-five years. My mother was a "have not." She moved with him for his tenure-track job when she was pregnant with me, then proceeded to teach at half a dozen different colleges in the area over the next several years. Her job prospects seemed always to be subject to the whims of—and I'm being charitable here—unstable departmental personalities.

My parents received their PhDs from the same acclaimed university, but my mother was never offered tenure after she began teaching. Instead, tired of this itinerant academic life, she decided to become an entrepreneur. She saw a need for a think tank devoted to local public policy issues, and she started it. She did the fund-raising, the research, the writing, and, when the time came, the hiring of additional staff. Despite her lack of tenure, she has never been afraid, as they say, "to speak truth to power." And there were plenty of times during the past twenty-five years when her think tank's future and her own position were in doubt.

But my father's tenure meant that there would always be at least one salary coming in.

The effects of tenure on the academic labor market were visible to me in the form of my parents' friends too: Couples who were forced into long-distance relationships so that one spouse could maintain a tenured position in the middle of nowhere while the other spouse went to find a job in a different city. Former students of my parents who were pushed off the long (and growing longer) road to a doctoral degree when they stopped to get married and start a family. The men and women who had already lost one tenure bid, who were trying to publish something—*anything*—to offer to another school's tenure committee.

I am both an insider and an outsider to this world. I always knew that the institution of tenure had a profound effect on those pursuing it, those who received it, and those who never won that academic gold medal. It made many keep their heads down and their mouths closed. After that, it made a few bolder, some more reckless, but many never hoisted the Jolly Roger at all. They remained as meek and eager to please as ever.

Until recently I wasn't sure whether the idiosyncratic promotion rules of the academy actually mattered to students, though. Sure, I knew that tenure had protected some mediocre faculty members—and a few

downright terrible ones. But if people with PhDs thought tenure was
the best way to promote quality in their profession, who was I to argue?

In truth, though, academics themselves have not spent much energy
reflecting on this issue. For all the new fields of inquiry out there, from
medical ethics to business ethics—the study of which is often done by
academics—there seems to be little in the way of higher-education ethics. It's time for faculty to take a hard look at their promotion system
to see whether it is helping or hindering higher education. What does
tenure have to do with the sort of experience colleges and universities
owe their students? How can faculty make a college education more coherent? How can they teach subjects that are both timeless and relevant?
How can they give students a broad range of perspectives in a particular
discipline? How can they make sure that the best professors are placed
in front of the greatest number of young people? How can they make
sure that good teachers are produced at all?

During a recent visit from my father, I received in the mail for review,
unsolicited, a six-hundred-page biography of an obscure literary figure.
My father picked up the book and wondered aloud who could possibly
want to read so much on such a subject. Then he asked how the author
could support himself on advances or royalties writing this kind of
thing. Publishers aren't supporting the author, I told him. Students are.
"Ten bucks says the guy has an academic appointment somewhere." As
my father turned to the jacket flap, he began to look a little sheepish. But
I didn't ask for the money.

My parents have given me many priceless things, but high among
them is steering me toward the best professors in college. Many schools
would have parents and students believe that the value of an education
relies entirely on how much the student makes of the opportunities
that universities and colleges provide. This type of rhetoric is sprinkled
throughout university brochures. But the idea that we should expect
seventeen-year-olds to figure out how to get a proper education—how
to spend their time and money wisely in the vast maze of academe—is
worse than ridiculous. It's a con game made to suit the interests of the

tenured faculty who would prefer to write obscure tomes rather than teach broad introductory classes to freshmen.

When we talk about the concept of a college acting "in loco parentis," the common understanding is that some administrator is enforcing a 10 p.m. curfew. But it used to mean that the folks in charge of universities put together a coherent educational program for students. Now they just leave it to the kids to make it up as they go along, all the while putting up the smokescreen that they are giving kids "the freedom to explore."

I was lucky enough not to need anyone acting in loco of my parentis. But it is my sincerest hope that we can return to an era where you don't need expert advice to get a good college education—preferably before my own children start college in fifteen years. Changing the tenure system is the first step in that process.

# Acknowledgments

A number of wise people agreed to be interviewed for this book, and their names are sprinkled throughout the pages that follow. But there were a few whose counsel I sought over and over. Anne Neal, Richard Vedder, Ben Wildavsky, John Miller, Richard Boris, and Mark Schneider have been invaluable resources. My colleagues at the *Wall Street Journal* were a source of inspiration as well, particularly Erich Eichman, who commented helpfully on the earliest formulations of my argument.

I owe a tremendous debt of gratitude to the Searle Trust and the Rupe Foundation for their support of this book, and to Ivan R. Dee for his thoughtful editing. Thanks also to my agent Jim Levine for his efforts on this book's behalf as well as Christine Whelan and Christine Rosen for their help and advice.

People often compare writing a book to having a child. I don't know that there's much truth to that, except to say that I've found a supportive husband good for both ventures. I've been blessed with a wonderful family. Jason, Emily, and Simon are the reason I sit down at my computer every morning and the best part of putting it away at night.

*N. S. R.*
*New Rochelle, New York*
*January 2011*

*"Today, class, I'm proud to announce my tenure."*

# 1

# A New Look at an Old Question

In November 2009, as a consequence of my earlier writings on education, I appeared on a panel in Washington, D.C., that was convened to discuss accountability in higher education. I was the sole objector to tenure—the system whereby after seven years at a particular institution, college professors are voted up or out. Either they are offered a permanent position or asked to leave. My fellow panelists—among them a representative of the American Association of University Professors and one from the National Research Council—roundly criticized me for my position. These two insisted not only that tenure is the best protector of a professor's right to teach and research freely but also that every professor, no matter his discipline—from "nutrition studies" to "security and protective services"—needed such a shield. They also labeled as a myth the notion that tenure insulates academics who are lazy or incompetent.

Very little of the discussion was surprising—that is, until I stepped down from the dais and returned to the table where I had been sitting. At which point, my fellow panelist, the middle-aged woman from the National Research Council, leaned over to me and said, "Of course, if I were starting my own university, I wouldn't have tenure."

By that point the crowd had disbursed, the microphones were turned off, and everyone had gone to refill their coffee cups. I felt as if I had just participated in some kind of elaborate academic kabuki dance. I had performed the role of outsider criticizing the institution because, of course, I didn't understand its true importance, while the insiders circled the wagons (if you'll permit a mixed metaphor) and repeated the same arguments they had been making for more than half a century. Even the reporter from *Inside Higher Ed* was bored by the whole discussion, calling my criticisms "time-honored" (read: familiar).

When I first began calling people to interview them about tenure in the fall of 2008, my requests were met with yawns. Many of the academics who agreed to speak with me would offer what I found to be a somewhat incoherent set of propositions. On the one hand I was told that tenure was the best way to protect the right of professors to speak and write freely. On the other hand I was told that tenure was already on its way out, so there was no point in arguing about it.

The second proposition certainly has some truth to it. The institution of tenure has experienced a severe decline in recent years. Tenured and tenure-track professors made up 55 percent of all faculty in 1970, 1975, and 1980. By 2003, they declined to 41 percent. Current estimates now put them at less than a third of the total. Not only are most full-time professors off the tenure track, but almost half of all college faculty are actually part-timers.

Tenure's fate, though, is hardly sealed. The American Association of University Professors (AAUP) is demanding that universities "convert" the bulk of their adjunct positions into tenure-track jobs. And powerful unions like the American Federation of Teachers (AFT) are pushing to mandate that a certain percentage of public university faculty (they often mention the figure 75 percent) be tenured or placed on the tenure track. If these mandates are written into bargaining contracts, tenure could be ubiquitous for the long haul.

Would this be a worthwhile development? It seems like most denizens of the ivory tower are rather uninterested in debating this proposition. Is there anything new to say here?

If media coverage of the issue is any indicator, the answer is yes. During the summer of 2010 the tenure issue began to heat up again.

The *New York Times* conducted two online forums: "What If Tenure Dies?" and "The Professors Who Won't Retire." *Slate*'s Christopher Beam wrote a piece called "Finishing School: The Case for Getting Rid of Tenure," and *Atlantic* editor Megan McArdle wrote "Tenure, an Idea Whose Time Has Gone." Even some academics are getting back into it. September 2010 saw the publication of Mark Taylor's *Crisis on Campus*. Taylor, head of Columbia University's religion department, made waves in 2009 when he argued in a *New York Times* op-ed for the abolition of tenure. And the eminent historian Andrew Hacker also published a book (coauthored by *New York Times* reporter Claudia Dreifus) called *Higher Education?*, which suggests that tenure "cannot be shown to be needed for, let alone enhance, good teaching or research. On the contrary," the authors write, "it diminishes both those endeavors." A few of tenure's defenders in the academy are also back in full force. Cary Nelson, president of the AAUP, came out with a book called *No University Is an Island*, which offers a full-throated defense of the institution. And Ellen Schrecker, historian of the McCarthy era, suggests that the rise of nontenured faculty will push our universities back toward the repression of the 1950s.

One reason tenure has returned as a popular topic seems to be economics. When we read headlines about skyrocketing college tuition in an era when the price of most everything else has remained stable or plummeted, we rightly become suspicious. According to a survey in February 2010 by the National Center on Public Policy and Higher Education, 60 percent of Americans say that colleges today act more like a business, concentrating on the bottom line rather than on the educational experience of students. This number has increased by 5 percentage points from 2009 to 2010 and by 8 percentage points since 2007.

Americans historically have tended to have very warm feelings about higher education—I heard one pollster compare asking about colleges to asking about mom and apple pie—but that may be changing. In recent years the excesses of higher education—from colleges' risky (but for a time, high-return) investment strategies to the gourmet food of their cafeterias and their elaborate gym facilities to their seeming inability to graduate many students in a reasonable amount of time—have set off alarm bells among parents and taxpayers.

And tenure hasn't been popular with the public for a while. A 2007 Zogby poll found that 65 percent of respondents agreed with this statement: "A professor who does not have tenure is more motivated to do a good job than one who does have tenure." A 2006 poll by the American Association of University Professors found that more than two-thirds of the public thinks tenure should be modified, and 13 percent think it should be eliminated.

Truth be told, tenure is not the reason why college costs so much. Expanding bureaucracies, luxurious facilities, remedial education, and a third-party payer system are more likely culprits. But tenure is certainly a symbol of the academic excesses that the public sees. Tenured professors do appear insulated from the vagaries of the market. They do seem unaccountable to the public and to parents and students. In an era when people change jobs an average of ten times just between the ages of eighteen and thirty-eight, the system of tenure seems anomalous. And when the unemployment rate hovers around 10 percent, tenure can seem outrageous.

But maybe it's unfair to judge the academy according to the economy surrounding it. In an article in the journal *Academic Questions*, University of Virginia English professor Paul Cantor once cautioned against applying the principles of the free market to higher education, which, he says, bears "little or no resemblance to the free market." He rightly notes, "Given the overwhelmingly bureaucratic character of American higher education today, and especially the way even private institutions are tied into federal and state bureaucracies, it is quixotic to think that personnel decisions can be placed on a market basis while the rest of the academic world remains unchanged. One cannot operate a free market island in the middle of a sea of bureaucracy." This is still the case. Our government contributes more to higher education now than ever, though it is now a smaller percentage of what it costs for colleges to educate students.

Others argue that academia bears more resemblance to the market than we may be willing to admit. There is a product, there are customers, and when things get too expensive, people look for other, cheaper alternatives. At any rate, even sectors of the economy in which a free market exists do not operate with the brutal efficiency we tend to assume. Academia is not the only profession in which men and women can presume indefinite employment. As John Silber, former president of Boston University, wrote in a chapter he contributed to a book called *The Tenure Debate*, surgeons "have tenure in the sense that they have a right to continue the practice of surgery indefinitely—a right virtually impossible to rescind, barring criminal acts." Lawyers continue at a firm even if they are less productive or less competent than they used to be. They may have a salary reduction, but they're rarely tossed out on the street. One needn't be a highly educated professional to have this deal. Silber continues, "We also know that in every business minor and major failings are tolerated at all levels, from executives to janitors. Except in times of severe financial strain, corporations and family businesses retain their employees by managing to overlook or resign themselves to their various shortcomings." The longer one is employed, the greater the presumption of continued employment.

The problem is with the way universities have applied these principles, Silber argues. As every academic likes to point out, tenure was never supposed to be a job for life. "Nothing in the concept of tenure precludes firing," Silber writes. "Tenure precludes only capricious or arbitrary firing." Professors like to blame "weak-willed" administrators for their inability to get rid of lazy or incompetent colleagues. They suggest that administrators don't use the kinds of carrots and sticks that are available to them—from salary increases to office assignments—that could get more professors to do their jobs better.

But it would be unreasonable to suggest that the temperament of administrators is the problem; the system seems to be broken in so many places. Silber suggests that it was the AAUP's insistence on the seven-year "up-or-out" rule that has ruined the system of tenure. "The

seven-year rule no longer serves as the dividing line between proba-
tionary and tenured employment. It has become, instead, the line that
divides probation from sinecure."

In fact, the sinecures afforded to the American faculty are probably
among the least significant problems with tenure. The tenure process,
which to a greater extent than ever rests on a professor's research rather
than his teaching qualifications, is what is eroding American higher
education from the inside out. The teaching of students suffers. There
is more publication than ever, but the subjects of academic books and
journal articles are narrower than before, often more trivial, and always
filled with jargon.

Tenure and promotion decisions at the university are decided almost
entirely by the faculty themselves and decided on the basis of research,
not teaching. The public's suspicion of tenure goes beyond the idea of a
sinecure for faculty. It also rests on the vague and seemingly irrelevant
standards by which professors are judged.

So, who should judge the quality of faculty, and how should they
be judged? "The key difference between the academic and the business
worlds, which many would-be reformers forget," writes Cantor, "is
that private enterprise has a relatively objective basis for judging the
performance of business executives." It is true that we can't really judge
professors based on how much money they make the university since
most professors are not attracting students (or even research grants) on
an individual basis. If research and publication are the basis for judgment, only other experts in the field can judge a faculty member. They
must be sufficiently knowledgeable to understand and appreciate (or
not appreciate) the contribution a colleague has made to the discipline.

But how do we judge the quality of teaching? The debate over the
worth of student evaluations continues to rage. Professors almost uniformly find them useless—and many are—but what other objective
measures are there? Many faculty report that there is simply no systematic way to evaluate teaching. We know good teaching when we see it,

they say. Faculty may occasionally have a colleague sit in on one of their classes before a tenure decision. But this evaluation is cursory at best.

It is not unusual to have members of a profession act as judge of one another. Doctors are best able to evaluate the skills of other doctors. The same is true for lawyers or even craftsmen. (A carpenter will point out flaws in another carpenter's work that a homeowner might never have noticed.) But the things that make them good are generally the things that patients, clients, and customers are also looking for.

The criteria by which faculty have chosen to judge one another, by contrast, are not relevant to most undergraduate students. College professors have abused this privilege of judging themselves to the point where their role in the process should be drastically reduced. With each passing year, more faculties whose missions are ostensibly to teach undergraduates require greater and greater levels of publication in order to achieve tenure. Older professors demand piles of articles and books from younger faculty that they themselves never would have accomplished. And the criteria required for tenure cannot just be tweaked. Tenure is a static system of promotion, and teaching is a dynamic activity, improved by steady feedback. Teaching this year's class well won't help next year's class. Faculty must be regularly evaluated in order to measure teaching quality.

The problems that occur once professors are tenured are not limited to laziness or incompetence. Once professors achieve tenure they continue in earnest to pursue ever-narrower research interests. We have now reached the point where academic departments are a haphazard collection of specialists who happen to have offices along the same hallway. Senior faculty want to teach upper-level seminars that align with their research interests rather than large introductory classes that might help undergraduates get a sense of a subject. Tenured faculty have pulled colleges away from core curricula to suit their own intellectual pursuits, thus denying experienced teachers to the students who need their efforts most. They have instituted a kind of intellectual conformity in most disciplines that is most obvious to the public when it comes to politics. But the problem goes far beyond the ivory tower leaning left. One academic parent of a physics professor told me that he knew if he didn't take a particular approach to string theory, he would be denied tenure and ousted from the university.

To fill in the gaps—that is, to do the real work of teaching—colleges have "adjunctified" themselves, using part-time faculty, graduate students, or others hired on a semester-to-semester basis. These faculty—who sometimes work at more than one campus, often earn less than minimum wage, and generally don't get benefits or even an office—turn out to be harmful to students' educational experience and even their graduation rates. And these adjuncts are treated as second-class citizens by their senior colleagues. The system of tenure was supposed to protect academia as a "profession." Instead it has worsened conditions for those on the bottom rungs of the academic ladder.

For faculty, meanwhile, the desire to get tenure has eclipsed all other goals. When Amy Bishop shot and killed three of her fellow professors at the University of Alabama at Huntsville, commentators immediately began to wonder whether it was related to the fact that she had recently been denied tenure. As it turned out, she had a violent past as well. Still, David Perlmutter, who writes a professional advice column for the *Chronicle of Higher Education*, used the occasion to call the situation facing aspiring professors "a perfect storm: a medieval system of bureaucracy, a set of rising expectations for performance and productivity, and a generation of young faculty members who fantasize about having a quasi-normal domestic life."

In a "Modern Love" column for the *New York Times*, one English professor recently compared the situation that she and her husband faced in trying to both get tenure simultaneously to Romeo and Juliet. When Caroline Bicks called her mother to tell her that her husband had lost his tenure bid, Bicks describes her reaction: "'What should I tell people?' she asked. It was as if he'd died under unseemly circumstances. And in a way he had. When you're denied tenure anywhere but at a few elite institutions, it's virtually impossible to get another tenure-track job. You're academic roadkill."

If the tenure system has failed students and failed the bulk of professors, defenders of tenure nonetheless ask, "What is the alternative?" Cantor warns that those who oppose tenure are "asking us to buy a pig in a poke."

The most promising alternative is multi-year renewable contracts, which are offered with much greater administrative input and not just by vote of a department. But faculty bristle at giving administrators more power. Cantor says that though he doesn't always respect the decisions of his faculty colleagues, they seem "positively Solomonic" when compared with those of administrators.

Cantor's complaint is an old and a feeble one. As the sociologists Christopher Jencks and David Riesman wrote in their 1968 survey of colleges and universities, *The Academic Revolution*, "administrators are today more concerned with keeping their faculty happy than with placating any other single groups. They are also, in our experience, far more responsive to students and more concerned with the inadequacies and tragedies of student life than the majority of faculty." In other words, they can be relied on to care more about teaching than professors ever would.

When pressed, many faculty, including Cantor, will say that tenure is necessary only for research schools. Other observers will add that we have too many research schools these days. Interestingly, professors at the very top of the profession, those who are apparently most deserving of tenure, actually don't care about it.

A senior administrator at one of the top private research universities told me he recently convened a group of a dozen or so of his most prestigious faculty and asked them two questions: "Should tenure exist?" And "In ten years, will it exist?" To the first question the group assembled unanimously answered no. To the second, all but one said yes. This is not exactly a ringing endorsement of higher education's ability to ensure quality.

Shortly after he took office, President Obama laid out his goals for higher education, which included asking "every American to commit to at least one year more of higher education or career training." He told the public that the federal government "will provide the support necessary for you to complete college and meet a new goal: by 2020, America will once again have the highest proportion of college graduates in the world."

Whatever one thinks about the goal of sending everyone to college, there is no question that making higher education universal will change the nature of it. What will distinguish college education from elementary and secondary education? Teacher tenure in those institutions has protected mediocrity across the country, and just about everyone knows it. A 2010 survey conducted by Harvard's Program on Education Policy and Governance (PEPG) and the journal *Education Next* found that Americans oppose tenure for schoolteachers by a two-to-one margin.

As college and university enrollment grows, these institutions need to put in place systems that will ensure a quality undergraduate education. Tenure, as we can see from our faltering public schools, is not the way to do that.

In 1951 Mary McCarthy published her classic campus novel *The Groves of Academe*. The mock epic is a story of how one professor, Henry Mulcahy, manages to convince his colleagues at a self-described "progressive college" that his teaching contract has not been renewed because the president has learned of his affiliation with the Communist Party.

At a meeting between the president, Maynard Hoar, and a couple of the colleagues who are supporting Mulcahy, the president begins to wonder why this professor has come under the impression that he deserves job security. Academics, he says, "are essentially public servants spiced with a dash of the rebel. Hence the common fixation on tenure; we feel that we serve for life like civil service employees." But then Hoar, a many-decade veteran of campus politics, starts to speculate:

I've fought all my life . . . for better teaching conditions, more benefits, recognition of seniority along trade-union lines, and yet sometimes I wonder whether we're on the right track, whether as creative persons we shouldn't live with more daring. Can you have creative teaching side by side with this preoccupation with security, with the principle of regular promotion and recognition of seniority? God knows in big universities, this system has fostered a great many academic barnacles. . . . Suppose we allowed Henry tenure, would it furnish him with the freedom he needs to let that tense personality of his expand and grow or would he settle down to the grind and become another old fossil? I don't know the answer.

Oh, President Hoar, yes, you do. We all do.

" YOUR WIFE HASN'T BROKEN THE LAW, PROFESSOR —
SHE CAN LEAVE YOU EVEN IF YOU <u>DO</u> HAVE TENURE. "

# 2

# The Battle Cry of Academic Freedom

Like Gulliver tied down by the Lilliputians, the large, serious figure pictured on the flyer has been muzzled and fenced in by people much smaller than he is. The flyer is an advertisement for the second annual conference of the Frederic Ewen Academic Freedom Center—and one needn't spend much time at the gathering to understand the picture's meaning. Today's university professor is restrained by innumerable little tyrants—state legislatures, religious organizations, right-wing interest groups, the CIA, and the American public.

On a cool morning in April 2009, with sheets of rain falling over the windows, forty or so people huddled in a conference room at New York University across the street from Washington Square. After some last-minute fiddling with a video screen, Stuart Ewen, a professor of history, sociology, and media studies at the City University of New York, stepped to the podium. He recalled his admiration—even as a child—for his Uncle Frederic, who resigned from his position teaching English at Brooklyn College in 1952 after refusing to testify before the House Un-American Activities Committee. He then devoted the next several years to putting on theatrical performances featuring actors who had been blacklisted for their alleged Communist ties.

These days the center launched in Frederic Ewen's honor is devoted to exposing what its founders see as a modern-day return to McCarthyism.

Among other initiatives Stuart Ewen mentions, the center is working with lawyers defending the Guantanamo Bay detainees to "archive all CIA web documents, all legal files, and collect oral history related to Guantanamo."

It's not made clear what this project has to do with academic freedom per se, but Alison Bernstein, the day's keynote speaker and a vice president at the Ford Foundation, explains that academic freedom tends to come under greater attack more in times of war and recession. We are in a bad way now, she warns, with both events occurring simultaneously.

The room sits rapt, as only a group of academics can when there is a representative of the Ford gravy train present. Here are just a few of the perpetrators who Bernstein claims are trying to exert influence over what college professors can say both inside the classroom and out: the Catholic order Opus Dei, "anti-evolution groups," "groups that want to cut off funding for those who are openly criticizing Israel," and organizations that oppose affirmative action.

And then, Berstein intones ominously, there is "philanthropy's role" in this crackdown. Lee Bass's $20 million gift to Yale in 1991 for a program in Western civilization (a gift that was returned four years later after the university acknowledged that it was not being used) as well as chairs at various prominent universities sponsored by the John M. Olin Foundation are "threats to academic freedom," according to the representative of the third-largest foundation in the United States.

Ford, Bernstein is quick to point out, funds only programs that encourage free expression on campus. She cites, for instance, Ford's 2005 "Difficult Dialogues" initiative, which offered campuses $100,000 each to host conversations about "fundamentalism and secularism, racial and ethnic relations, the Middle East conflict, religion and the university, sexual orientation, and academic freedom."

Such dialogues are, one might observe, not difficult at all on most campuses because the outcomes are agreed upon. Secularism is superior to fundamentalism; white people are to blame for racial tensions; the Middle East conflict could be solved if Israel weren't bent on massacring innocent Palestinians; religion doesn't really belong on campus, unless it's Buddhism; sexual orientation has genetic roots, and all orientations are morally equivalent.

And what's the party line on academic freedom? It has suffered because of the Bush administration's war on terror. Or, as Bernstein puts it, "the war *of* terror." Only a few months into the Obama administration, she is circumspect about the likelihood that the president will reverse all these policies before they have done permanent damage.

Perhaps the only surprising part of Bernstein's presentation is the extent to which she argues that the American people themselves are directly responsible for what she sees as the oppressive atmosphere on campus. "Thanks to technology," she sighs, "the ability of average citizens to critique and demean faculty grows daily."

Just to be clear, here was a representative of the Ford Foundation, the sugar daddy of modern liberalism, complaining that innovations like twenty-four-hour news stations and the Internet have made universities *too* transparent.

If only the public didn't demand such accountability from universities, she seemed to be saying, professors would truly be free to pursue their scholarly interests. The outrage is that citizens are calling their legislators, wanting, for example, to know why tax dollars were being spent to pay University of Colorado professor Ward Churchill, who called the 9/11 victims "little Eichmanns." Or imagine the gall of those Columbia University alumni demanding that the university president censure Nicholas De Genova, who, at a campus anti-war rally, expressed his hope that U.S. troops experience "a million Mogadishus."

Accountability, in this estimation, is anathema to academic freedom.

If you ask a professor why he needs tenure, the first words out of his mouth will undoubtedly be some variation of this phrase: "to guarantee academic freedom." Believe me, I've tried this dozens, if not hundreds, of times. I have asked professors on both ends of the political spectrum and those whose work falls squarely in the middle. They have all given me the same response, at least to start. If professors don't have a guaranteed job for life (or what usually amounts to it), the argument goes, they will not be able to speak or write freely. Those with unpopular views—or views that upset the administration or the trustees or other members of the faculty—will be run off campus.

But many Americans might wonder why academic freedom is a principle worth defending anyway. Don't some radical faculty members deserve to be run off campus? Why aren't college faculty subject to the same kind of scrutiny by customers (that is, parents and students) and the general public that other sorts of professionals are? Does tenure really protect academic freedom? And, if we may be so bold, how important is academic freedom to the duties that most academics today perform?

The idea that tenure protects academic freedom is "an article of faith," says David Kirp, professor of public policy at the University of California, Berkeley. "It needs to be justified." Let me add to Kirp's challenge. It is not simply that tenure needs to be justified. We must first answer the question of who needs academic freedom in the first place.

Let's explore several groups of professors for whom academic freedom is largely unnecessary. The extension of academic freedom to people teaching basic courses, like freshman composition and elementary math, or vocational courses like business or nutrition, produces a lack of consistency and quality control in higher education.[1] But there are also professors teaching in the physical sciences, as well as in a variety of vocational areas and in area, ethnic, and gender studies, for whom academic freedom is not at all necessary. Granting it to them anyway, as we shall see, only invites trouble.

---

1. Professors teaching these subjects often become dissatisfied with the curriculum and decide to use the mantle of academic freedom to put their own special stamp on these courses, regardless of its relevance.

Until the early twentieth century, tenure was really a de facto arrangement. It had little to do with academic freedom and was intended mostly to protect the economic security of a group of people who devoted long years to training for a job that didn't provide much remuneration. For that matter, tenure wasn't a particularly unusual arrangement throughout the workplace. In 1950 most people worked for the same company for their entire lifetime. It didn't seem unreasonable for professors to have a similar deal.

Early on, professors didn't need tenure to protect their academic freedom, because academic freedom wasn't much of an issue. No doubt some intellectuals found themselves on the wrong side of public sentiment, but they were the exceptions. Most of the first American colleges were religious. Sometimes they were devoted specifically to training clergy. Many simply took a religious vision as the foundation for studies of the secular world. The goals of such schools were well illustrated in a 1643 brochure explaining Harvard's purpose: "To advance Learning and perpetuate it to Posterity; dreading to leave an illiterate Ministry to the Churches."

If this is a school's stated mission, the question of who deserves to teach there is not open-ended. When lines were crossed—that is, when faculty engaged in one sort of heresy or another—they were dismissed. The rules were made abundantly clear from the beginning.

In the nineteenth century, the conflicts between scholars and university benefactors began to multiply. A few factors drove this trend. First, religious institutions began to receive a smaller percentage of their funding from denominational churches, and university scholars and administrators sought to compete with secular schools by shedding their parochial identities. Second, more and more universities saw money coming in from business interests, who were hoping to see scientific advances that would bear fruit for the American economy. And third, President Lincoln signed the Morrill Act in 1862, which provided the basis for "land-grant universities," making the state and federal governments major benefactors of higher education in a way they hadn't been before.

Despite the money they poured into the system, America's clergy, businessmen, and politicians were not altogether happy with the results. The faculty had their own ideas about what they wanted to study and how. And they didn't much care for outside interference. As Bruce Smith, Jeremy Mayer, and A. Lee Fritschler note in their recent book *Closed Minds: Politics and Ideology in American Universities*, the universities "wanted patronage, but found it difficult to live with the patrons."

The first significant conflict along these lines occurred in 1894. Richard Ely, who directed the University of Wisconsin's School of Economics, Politics, and History, found himself accused by the state superintendent of education of inciting agitation of organized labor and encouraging people who were not unionized to get cracking. Ely, who was studying what we might now call the "root causes" of violent labor unrest, was tried in a three-day hearing that was later dramatized on *Profiles in Courage*, the 1960s television series. He was absolved of the charges. The university regents concluded, "In all lines of academic investigation it is of utmost importance that the investigator should be absolutely free to follow the indications of truth wherever they may lead."

Actually it was one of the regents, John M. Olin—the same man whose foundation was accused by Ford's Alison Bernstein of violating the principles of academic freedom—who insisted that the regents' conclusion be used "to do the University a great service." A plaque at the school now reads, "Whatever may be the limitations which trammel inquiry elsewhere, we believe that the great state University of Wisconsin should ever encourage that continual and fearless sifting and winnowing by which alone the truth can be found."

Ely's case is still celebrated today, not only for its inspirational words. It was also a rare event in the history of higher education. Despite the simmering tensions between patrons and professors, few faculty members in the nineteenth or early twentieth centuries ever suffered dismissal as a result of controversial scholarship. And few politicians or members of the public demanded it.

Edward Ross, a Stanford University economist, was not as lucky as Ely. Ross, who favored a ban on Asian immigration, pushed for municipally owned utilities, and supported socialist Eugene Debs for president, found himself on the wrong side of the school's benefactor, Mrs. Leland Stanford. Her husband had made his money in railroads and gave the seed money to start the university. In 1900, she wrote to the university's president, David Starr Jordan, "When I take up a newspaper . . . and read the utterances of Professor Ross and realize that a professor of the Leland Stanford Junior University thus steps aside, and out of his sphere, to associate with the political demagogues of this city . . . it brings tears to my eyes. I must confess I am weary of Professor Ross, and I think he ought not to be retained by Stanford University."

On November 16, 1900, the *New York Times* published an account of Ross's departure from the university: "In his formal letter of resignation, he intimated that he was being forced out of the university by Mrs. Stanford who had taken exceptions to statements made by him in his public addresses on sociological and economic question [*sic*]." Jordan denied that the benefactor's wishes had anything to do with Ross's resignation, but the dots were not hard to connect.

Unlike some of its cousins back East, Stanford was not originally a religious institution. It was founded on the German model of a "research university." This new model, which came to the American shores in the nineteenth century, had two distinct features. One was that its faculty was directed to pursue knowledge free from any "proprietary" strictures. According to this approach, no benefactor of the institution, whether a religious leader or a businessman or a politician, could determine the direction of the faculty's scholarship. In other words, the founders of this system seemed to build into it a lack of accountability.

The second feature of the research university was that professors were no longer simply educating students in classical texts with a view to making them good people or good citizens. Rather, faculty at these new institutions were conceived of as experts. They were supposed to add to the general pool of knowledge available to mankind and use that knowledge to improve society. Under the old model of the proprietary institution, of course, the school administrators could still decide what sorts of research and teaching fell afoul of the institutional mission. But under the new model, only faculty colleagues familiar with a particular discipline could determine the bounds for research.

The research university made some sense for professors studying the physical sciences. The nineteenth century began with the invention of the steam locomotive and the stethoscope and ended with the development of the internal combustion engine and germ theory. Scientific knowledge was becoming more specialized and more difficult for the average person to understand.

The implications of the new research university for professors in the social sciences and humanities were harder to comprehend. After all, what did it mean that professors of sociology or history or English were supposed to add to the store of society's knowledge? Is our twenty-first-century understanding of Shakespeare inherently superior to that of the seventeenth century? Should we count on modern professors of political science to improve American government? Do they understand our politics better than, say, the authors of the Federalist Papers?

The answer of the era's progressives was an unqualified yes. Herbert Croly, one of the leading progressive thinkers, wrote of the need in government for a "permanent body of experts in social administration" whose task would be to "promote individual and social welfare." For our own good, the progressives argued, we needed to protect the rights of professors to engage in any kind of scholarship they and their fellow experts deemed necessary. By this understanding, their "scholarship" extended far beyond the bounds of the university. They were to be public intellectuals. And yet their expertise meant that these men could not be held accountable by the *public*, who knew nothing of such complex matters. Thanks to the progressives' understanding of the role of professors—as experts advising government and the public, and as professionals uniquely qualified in their fields—faculty today can justify almost any statement as speech deserving of the protections of academic freedom. Observers of higher education often wonder how academic freedom, intended as a barrier around the classroom or the research lab, became a sort of bubble that protects professors wherever they may wander. The wheels were set in motion early on.

In firing Edward Ross, Stanford had plainly violated the new rules of the higher-education game. A year later seven Stanford professors resigned in protest of the university's actions. Among them was Arthur O. Lovejoy, a philosophy professor.

Fifteen years later Lovejoy, along with the famed progressive educator John Dewey, formed the American Association of University Professors. The Declaration of Principles they issued remains a sort of biblical document among academics today. Here, for Dewey and his colleagues, was the crux of the matter: "To the degree that professional scholars, in the formation and promulgation of their opinions, are, or by the character of their tenure appear to be, subject to any motive other than their own scientific conscience and a desire for the respect of their fellow-experts, to that degree the university teaching profession is corrupted; its proper influence upon public opinion is diminished and vitiated; and society at large fails to get from its scholars, in an unadulterated form, the peculiar and necessary service which it is the office of the professional scholar to furnish."

As far as Dewey and his colleagues were concerned, if faculty found their teaching or writing or "outside" statements were being influenced by, say, their desire to hold on to their jobs, they didn't have much academic freedom. The AAUP issued a "restatement" of this idea in 1940.

In the second half of the twentieth century the AAUP has come to represent most of the country's faculty in one way or another, and the organization's pronouncements on academic freedom and tenure have come to be the law of the academic land. But there is still a lot of confusion about what academic freedom means. "The commentary on these AAUP statements is like the Talmud," jokes Martin Finkelstein, a professor of higher education at Seton Hall University. "So many people have attempted to do an exegesis on this or that aspect of the statement. But, for all of our discussion in the academy, I think we do a terrible job of articulating what we mean by academic freedom." Even Robert O'Neill, director of the Thomas Jefferson Center for the Protection of Free Expression at the University of Virginia and a member of the AAUP's Committee on Academic Freedom and Tenure, agrees that the organization has not done a very good job of explaining what all this means. "The formulation of a substantive principle of academic freedom is difficult," he tells me.

"Is it academic freedom," Finkelstein asks, "to teach anything you want when giving a course in freshman English?" What if the department has a syllabus that all the instructors are required to follow? "Is this an issue of academic freedom?" he wonders. This is a particularly important question for widely offered courses like freshman composition.

Indeed, Finkelstein's questions bring to mind the controversy a few years ago over a UC Berkeley course offering called "The Politics and Poetics of Palestinian Resistance." Listed as a "composition" class in the English department, the instructor explained, "This class takes as its starting point the right of Palestinians to fight for their own self-determination," and "Conservative thinkers are encouraged to seek other sections." As Erin O'Connor explained in her blog, *Critical Mass*, "politics seems to interest Cal's fall writing instructors more than writing does. Roughly twice as many courses promise to address politics—which they define, predictably and uniformly, in terms of race, class, gender, nation, ethnicity, ideology—than promise to address the craft and technique of writing. Many instructors seem to have forgotten entirely that they are teaching writing courses, and make no mention of writing at all in their descriptions of what students who take their class will do." Is it academic freedom to stray so far from the job you were hired to do?

Even the legal definition of academic freedom is in flux. As it pertains to private universities, the courts have traditionally considered that professors and administrators have a contract. And like any other employer, the university is required to live up to the terms of it. But if the contract says the institution is an evangelical Christian one and faculty should not say things that violate a particular church's teachings, then those who do, whether or not they have tenure, can be fired. Of course, there are professors who decide to run afoul of the rules anyway, and the AAUP has censured innumerable religious institutions—like Brigham Young University—for restricting the activities of its faculty members. Overall, though, private institutions seem to have plenty of autonomy from a legal perspective.

At public institutions, however, the matter is significantly more complex.[2] Oddly enough, the current precedent for determining what professors can say seems to be a 2006 Supreme Court case (*Garcetti v. Ceballos*) about a Los Angeles deputy district attorney, Richard Ceballos. While prosecuting a case for the district, Ceballos found inaccuracies in a warrant. In a memo to his superiors, he recommended dismissing the case. The department didn't take his recommendation, and he was subsequently called by the defense to testify in the case because he had undertaken a lengthy investigation of his own into the faulty warrant. Ceballos claimed his supervisors retaliated against him by, among other things, denying him a promotion. This, according to Ceballos, constituted a violation of his First Amendment rights—he was being punished for the words he used in his memo. The court held, though, "that when

---

2. Public university faculty are basically public employees. Since we don't want government to be in the business of censoring speech, public faculty have a wider latitude.

public employees make statements pursuant to their official duties, the employees are not speaking as citizens for First Amendment purposes, and the Constitution does not insulate their communications from employer discipline."

But surely the jobs of a professor and that of other public employees are different. Professors are not simply hired for the purpose of being government mouthpieces or to carry out the government's bidding, the way, say, a bureaucrat in a municipal department of public health might be asked to do. In other words, professors are not supposed to be instruments of the state. (Some libertarians would reasonably argue that this is the problem with public universities in the first place.) And if they are not instruments of the state, to whom are the professors accountable? Do taxpayers have any recourse when public university faculty go off the rails?

The Court briefly acknowledged the dilemma in applying the public-employee standard to university professors when it wrote, "We need not, and for that reason do not, decide whether the analysis we conduct today would apply in the same manner to a case involving speech related to scholarship or teaching."

But as it stands, the Court has not clarified what the decision does mean for professors. Rachel Levinson, general counsel for the American Association of University Professors, notes one important problem with the way the court has drawn the lines: "The paradox of *Garcetti* is that the more you know about something, the less you are protected for speaking about it." Levinson believes that this is "problematic for the faculty and the public interest as well." If a constitutional law professor wants to write a controversial op-ed about constitutional law, he won't be protected from retaliation by his employer; but if he wants to write one about the scientific proof for the existence of UFOs, the university has no claim against him. Levinson argues that the *Garcetti* decision actually means that professors' speech is protected *less* than that of the average American: "Do you give up the basic rights of being a citizen when you become a government employee?"

It's important to remember that the concerns raised by Levinson are still hypothetical. No university employment case has been decided by the highest court since *Garcetti*, and no tenured professor has had any of his speech restricted.

And while the Supreme Court has left things vague, some lower courts have taken up the issue of academic freedom, pushing things farther in the direction of the faculty. In 2003 five professors at the Metro College of Denver sued their employer, claiming that changes in the school handbook significantly altered the terms of their employment by making it easier to fire tenured professors. The state district court ruled for the college trustees. The decision was appealed—with the American Association of University Professors filing an amicus brief—and in 2007 a state appeals court ordered a new trial.

The AAUP argued in its brief that "depriving the tenured faculty of a preference in retention places the tenured faculty at greater risk of being singled out" because of an administrator's or trustee's dislike for his teaching or research, or for positions taken on issues off campus.

The results of that new trial came down in June 2009. Rather than simply deciding that the change in the handbook altered what was a "vested right" of the professors, Judge Norman D. Haglund ruled that "the public interest is advanced more by tenure systems that favor academic freedom over tenure systems that favor flexibility in hiring or firing." He also noted that "by its very nature, tenure promotes a system in which academic freedom is protected." In this ruling Judge Haglund purports to know the best governance policies for universities; he is also cementing in law the relationship between academic freedom and tenure.

Thus, in the course of the past hundred years or so, we've gone from tenure as a de facto system that gives poor academics a little economic security to a system where tenure is deemed by our courts to be in the public interest because it protects academic freedom. Despite this, we are still without a very good definition of academic freedom.

Perhaps the best way to proceed is by using a little common sense. Most Americans would probably agree that some courses in some subjects at some universities require professors to go out on a limb. Those faculty members will have to question accepted truths. They might say things that their colleagues don't agree with. They might write things in newspapers or academic journals that challenge the theories or conclusions of their disciplines. We should not fire those people for saying such things.

Perhaps, but higher education today looks a lot different than it did in John Dewey's time. Do all the new additions to our university menu mean we need to extend the protections of academic freedom to a whole bunch of new chefs?

Tenure, Stanley Fish writes in his book *Save the World on Your Own Time*, was not meant to protect off-the-cuff political statements outside the classroom but merely the freedom to teach and conduct research in one's own discipline without administrative interference. That is a kind interpretation of Dewey and his colleagues. One might have predicted this result of every word being protected by academic freedom once we invested professors with the status of experts on what is best for society. Still, when all is said and done, writes Fish in the *Chronicle of Higher Education*, "academic freedom is just a fancy name for being allowed to do your job, and it is only because that job has the peculiar feature of not having a pre-stipulated goal that those who do it must be granted a degree of latitude and flexibility not granted to the practitioners of other professions. That's why there's no such thing as 'corporate-manager freedom' or 'shoe-salesman freedom' or 'dermatologist freedom.'"

But here is the truth of the matter: More college teachers resemble dermatologists and corporate managers and shoe salesmen than ever before. I do not say this to insult them but merely to acknowledge this fact. The landscape of higher education has changed, and most courses have exactly what Fish calls a "pre-stipulated goal."

According to the Integrated Postsecondary Education Data System (IPEDS) compiled by the Department of Education, the total number of four-year degrees awarded during the 1970–1971 school year was 839,730. By 2005–2006 that number had jumped to 1,485,242, an increase of 77 percent. (The U.S. population grew by about half during the same time.) We are a wealthier country now. More of the American population can afford college, and more of us need it too. As factory jobs became a less reliable source of lifetime income, high school graduates looked to college to train themselves both for our information economy and our service economy. It is also true that K–12 education in America has experienced a decline. Some of the knowledge that young people used to receive in high school is now gained only through a college degree. Finally, apprenticeships are less common. That is, job skills that people used to learn under the watchful eye of a single skilled craftsman are now offered only in a formal setting.

The bottom line is that people who never used to go to college now find that they have to in order to train for good jobs. And so, not surprisingly, a significant portion of those additional degrees that colleges have added in the past few decades have been in vocational areas. Degrees in agriculture and natural resources doubled. Degrees in communications and related fields increased sevenfold. The number of degrees awarded in health sciences tripled. Parks, recreation, leisure, and fitness studies rose from 1,621 degrees in 1971 to 25,490 in 2006. As a percentage of degrees awarded, these vocational categories that once accounted for 10 percent of all four-year degrees grew to 22 percent. In fact, in the past twenty-five years vocational degrees made up 38 percent of the overall increase in four-year degrees.

There is no doubt that young people with these vocational degrees have contributed significantly to American prosperity. But these fields simply do not engage students in a search for ultimate truths. They all have "pre-stipulated goals" that are immediately obvious. One must ask, do we need to guarantee the academic freedom of professors engaged in teaching and studying "Transportation and Materials Moving," a field in which more than five thousand degrees were awarded in 2006?

Of course there are also plenty of what one might call vocational courses within nonvocational fields. Freshman composition, a requirement at almost every four-year institution in the country, does not demand that faculty members ask existential questions. Some will say that making judgments about the quality of writing is inherently subjective. But most college freshmen have yet to master even the most basic principles of thesis statements, rules of grammar and style, and research citations. If these courses are not fundamentally rigorous exercises in "how to" rather than "why," then the faculty teaching them haven't done their jobs. Yet it is increasingly common to hear disgruntled junior faculty complain that sticking to a required curriculum for these types of courses is a violation of their academic freedom. Some would rather teach Derrida, but that's not the purpose of the course.

In the Declaration of Principles, Dewey wrote that "if education is the cornerstone of the structure of society and progress in scientific knowledge is essential to civilization, few things can be more important than to enhance the dignity of the scholar's profession." There is no need to belittle or demean teachers of vocational subjects, but we would be kidding ourselves if we suggested that degrees in "family and consumer sciences" (20,775, all of them awarded in 2006) are "essential to civilization." We don't have to treat the people who teach them badly, but we also don't need to "enhance the dignity" of their positions by offering them job perks like tenure. Do professors of "security and protective services" (35,319 degrees) really need to be granted the freedom to make controversial statements in the interests of creating a better learning environment?

Many of the courses offered at the Metro College of Denver—the subject of the aforementioned lawsuit—fall into exactly this vocational category. Some of the courses taught this year by the five professors who sued include "American Baseball History" and "Business Statistics." The school even offers a nutrition major. These are all fields of study with fairly definitive answers. Faculty members don't really need the freedom to ask controversial questions in discussing them.

The idea sounds absurd, but when I brought up some of these disciplines at a panel at the American Enterprise Institute in 2009, I was told by Gary Rhoades, general secretary of the AAUP, that nutrition professors might have something controversial to say about the obesity epidemic, and protective services professors might have something controversial to say about our border policies.

When we tie ourselves in knots to make sure that professors of these vocational subjects are guaranteed their academic freedom, we are only asking for trouble. As Peter Berkowitz of the Hoover Institution rightly notes, "The more a college education is vocational, the less you need tenure." And the more we give people tenure when they don't need it, the more times we will end up defending the perfectly outrageous.

Take the case, for instance, of Arthur Butz, who has been teaching electrical engineering at Northwestern University for more than three decades now. In 1976, he published *The Hoax of the Twentieth Century: The Case Against the Presumed Extermination of European Jewry*, shortly after he received tenure. A couple of years ago, in interviews with the Iranian press, Butz was asked about Iranian president Mahmoud Ahmadinejad's views on the Holocaust: "I congratulate him on becoming the first head of state to speak out clearly on these issues and regret only that it was not a Western head of state," Butz offered.

For years Northwestern has been tacitly defending Butz's Holocaust denial as within the bounds of his "academic freedom." The protections of academic freedom have once again followed the professor out of the classroom. Obviously the Northwestern administration could be making more informed distinctions about how and where Butz should be protected. But why bother? Why does a professor of electrical engineering need protection in the first place? Was he going to go out on a limb with some untested idea about integrated circuit design and be subject to persecution at the hands of the university administration or board of trustees? No. The only occasions on which people in disciplines with "pre-stipulated goals" make use of their academic freedom is to stray from their field.

But, critics will ask, doesn't Butz have rights as a citizen of the United States to say whatever he wants? Sure, but he doesn't have the right to his job. If Butz were running a Fortune 500 company, do you think he'd be allowed to spout this nonsense? The board of directors would fire him in an instant. They couldn't revoke his citizenship, but they sure wouldn't have to pay him a salary. That's the kind of accountability that exists in other sectors of our economy.

In its 1915 statement, the AAUP founders discussed the case of "a proprietary school or college designed for the propagation of specific doctrines prescribed by those who have furnished its endowment." The writers were referring to the institutions of the time—those controlled by religious denominations, or the case of "a wealthy manufacturer [who] establishes a special school in a university in order to teach, among other things, the advantages of a protective tariff." In these cases, the authors conclude, "the trustees have a right to demand that everything be subordinated to that end."

The AAUP authors express no opinion about the "desirability of the existence of such institutions." If someone wants to fund a university for a particular end, that's fine. "But," they write, "it is manifestly important that they should not be permitted to sail under false colors. Genuine boldness and thoroughness of inquiry, and freedom of speech, are scarcely reconcilable with the prescribed inculcation of a particular opinion upon a controverted question."

Today the proprietary institution has returned. Take research scientists, who are increasingly entering into multimillion-dollar contracts with corporations. Unlike Edward Ross, the professor at Stanford who was fired for his political views, these faculty members are directly selling their services to pharmaceutical companies or firms engaged in biomedical research. The university itself often gets a cut of the deal, but the faculty are definitely at the bargaining table. And the corporations are often engaged in determining whether the results of the research are released, and how. If academic freedom means the ability to question not only the assumptions of a particular discipline but also the free flow of information gained from research and writing, then many faculty members seem to be selling their cherished principles.

Take, for example, the University of California. As Jennifer Washburn documents in her book *University, Inc.*, "From 1993 to 2003 . . . industry-sponsored research at the U.C. system grew 97 percent in real terms (from $65 million to $155 million)." In 1998 UC Berkeley signed a $25 million agreement with the pharmaceutical company Novartis. Under the agreement, Washburn writes, "Berkeley granted Novartis first right to negotiate licenses on roughly one-third of the [Department of Plant and Microbial Biology's] discoveries, including the results of research funded by Novartis, as well as projects funded by state and federal resources. It also granted the company unprecedented representation—two of five seats—on the department's research committee which determined how the money would be spent."

Of course, faculty objections to this arrangement followed. After all, it basically gave a private corporation a vested interest in, not to mention proprietary rights to, the research that was supposedly being conducted by impartial scientists. Still, 41 percent of the faculty in the College of Natural Resources, according to Washburn, "supported the agreement as signed."

And why wouldn't they? If they agreed to the corporations' terms, these professors would see the resources for their departments expanded, their prominence rise, and, presumably, a nice bump in their salaries too. But how far are they willing to go in acceding to the industry's terms? Washburn's research is eye-opening.

In another section of her book, she describes a team at the University of California, San Francisco, that signed a contract with the Immune Response Corporation to test the company's newly developed AIDS drug Remune. Three years into the testing, the researchers determined that the drug was ineffective, according to Washburn. When they went to write up the results, however, they noticed a clause in their contract with IRC saying that they couldn't use any of the raw data from their study in publications. This is not uncommon. One Harvard survey found that 88 percent of life science companies often require students and faculty to keep information confidential.

A few years ago Professor Donald Downs at the University of Wisconsin began to notice this tension between academic freedom and the desire of universities and professors themselves to gain corporate partners. His own university was about to sign a contract with Reebok, which would be the exclusive supplier of athletic attire for the university. And university employees would promise not to say anything negative about Reebok. (The concern, apparently, was that someone would comment on Reebok's labor practices. Nike had received bad publicity a few years earlier when some faculty members at the universities whose attire they were supplying accused the company of using sweatshop labor.) Downs recalls going to the chancellor and demanding that he excise this clause. "Once you have a gag order between a university and someone outside, you're playing with the devil," says Downs.

Some observers of higher education would come away with the impression that only administrators are engaged in this kind of solicitation. But, as Washburn notes, there are plenty of professors these days who are playing the role of corporate interest as well. They own their own companies and often use their undergraduate and graduate students as employees. The *Wall Street Journal* reported one MIT student who refused to hand in homework to one professor because he feared that doing so would violate his employment agreement with a company founded by another of his professors.

It is also important to note that research scientists, unlike many academics, are not hurting for money. The AAUP's original desire to ensure that academics have a degree of economic security to "enhance the dignity" of their profession is not a concern of this group. One need only look at recent reports on the apparently widespread practice of "ghostwriting" journal articles among some research scientists to realize how many professors seem to forget that their primary employers are universities, not pharmaceutical companies. As an editorial in the *Public Library of Science* journal explained the problem, "While readers expect and assume that the named academic authors on a paper carried out the piece of work and then wrote up their article or review informed by their professional qualifications and expertise, instead we see . . . 'ghostwriting': a writing company was commissioned to produce a manuscript on a piece of research to fit the drug company's needs and then a person was identified to be the 'author.'"

If professors and students choose to enter into commercial agreements with corporations, there is no law preventing them from doing so. Schools will have to negotiate for themselves whether they understand their faculty to be acting ethically. As the AAUP founders said, there is nothing wrong with these proprietary agreements per se.

But they do reveal a great deal about the value that university faculty place on academic freedom. If the price is right, they are happy to give it up. (One could imagine that humanities professors might feel the same, if only someone were willing to pay so much for a study of Chaucer.) Given this attitude among many research scientists, why should the public take their claims to academic freedom seriously? If they're voluntarily giving it up, should we really worry about taking it away?

Unlike many others in the academy, it turns out that professors in the physical sciences are subject to some standards of accountability. The market compensates the competent ones, not the incompetent ones. But these professors still don't seem to be answerable to the parents and taxpayers funding their academic salaries. Many of these faculty have simply arranged their workload and their careers in order to please their highest corporate bidders. But if their jobs as faculty members are not their priority, we don't need to offer them special protections as such.

Another change in the face of higher education over the past thirty years has been the expansion of "area, ethnic, cultural, and gender studies." Only 2,579 degrees were awarded in these areas in 1971. Today that number has tripled to 7,879. Unlike the vocational degrees, this increase has been felt most at the country's elite institutions. At universities that ranked in the top twenty-five in the *U.S. News and World Report* survey, degrees in these disciplines rose from an average of thirty-five per school in 1987 to seventy-three per school in 2006.

Like the vocational disciplines, the missions of these academic pursuits also have predetermined outcomes. As Mark Bauerlein of Emory University explains, in many cases "ideological content has drifted down to the fundamental norms of the discipline." Whether it's women's studies or black studies or queer studies, the entire premise of the discipline often rests on a political agenda. While the cases of departments with political agendas may be more difficult to sort out, they are certainly worth considering in the grand scheme of "academic freedom creep." Just as with the vocational disciplines, there is, in these areas, a growing sense that projects that are not strictly academic are not deserving of academic protections.

As Ellen Schrecker, a Yeshiva University historian, writes in her book *The Lost Soul of Higher Education*, political ends were the goals of the founders of these disciplines. Schrecker, who is herself sympathetic to these political goals, cites the historian David Hollinger, a Berkeley graduate student in the 1960s: "Life outside of the classes seemed to have become an all-day, half-the-night seminar involving everyone I knew discussing the meaning of the university and the life of the mind in relation to the rest of the world." Many faculty and students during that tumultuous period began to see the classroom as politics by other means. Proponents of black studies "viewed these programs," according to Schrecker, "as contributions to the ongoing struggle for racial justice, not as conventional academic courses of study." One early supporter of women's studies wrote, "What administrators didn't realize, of course, was that it was almost impossible to take a women's studies class, as scholarly as it might be, without developing a feminist consciousness."

Today the mission statements of these departments reflect those goals. At Berkeley the Department of African American Studies' mission "emerges out of a conviction that a sound understanding of the realities of the life and culture of persons of African descent in the United States cannot but take into account the legacies of colonialism, enslavement, the plantation, and migration." And at the State University of New York at New Paltz, the Department of Black Studies "seeks to define the Black experience from an African and Afro-American centered perspective rather than Euro-centric perspective." Courses include "Psychology of the Black Child," which "assumes that Black children are, in general, subject to forces that cause their psychological development to differ from that of the middle class American child studied in traditional child psychology courses."

"Political correctness represented the return of proprietary universities," says Donald Downs. They may not have religious goals or industrial ones, but they are pre-stipulated nonetheless. It is not merely that these departments approach African American studies from a particular perspective—an Africa-centered one in which blacks residing in America today are still deeply hobbled by the legacy of slavery. It's that course and department descriptions often appear to be a series of axes that faculty members would like to grind. Frequently these departments also insist that their professors engage in a particular political project.

Take the mission of Ohio State's department, where the faculty "contributes ideas for the formulation and implementation of progressive public policies with positive consequences for the black community." The distinction between academic researcher and policymaker is thus lost. The emphasis on "service learning," which has recently become all the rage in higher education, contributes to this trend. It means that faculty members are no longer simply engaged in teaching and learning and research. Rather, they are supposed to lead students into the field to accomplish particular "progressive public policies." (One imagines that Herbert Croly would have approved.)

A similar trend may be seen in women's studies departments (many of which have become gender studies departments in recent years, in order to include queer studies and the study of sexuality generally). At Columbia College in South Carolina the women's studies program "encourages students to advocate for social justice for women." At Iona College in New York the department is supposed to "promote social justice for women through the practical application of theory [and] . . . develop proactive responses to the differential impact of gender-based bias in the lives of women from diverse backgrounds and experiences."

And just like the case of African American studies, professors are not supposed to be engaged simply in policymaking. The endpoint of their academic study is also predetermined. Take, for example, the University of Rhode Island, where "the discipline of Women's Studies has a vision of a world free from sexism. By necessity, freedom from sexism must include a commitment to freedom from nationalism; class, ethnic, racial, and heterosexual bias; economic exploitation; religious persecution; ageism; and ableism. Women's Studies seeks to identify, understand, and challenge ideologies and institutions that knowingly or unknowingly oppress and exploit some for the advantage of others, or deny fundamental human rights." At Penn State the department "analyzes the unequal distribution of power and resources by gender." The Department of Sexuality Studies at Duke has as its "central emphasis" the "social construction of sexuality—that is, how sexuality is shaped by historical, social, and symbolic contexts."

But what if you believe, as many Americans do, that gender is not purely a "social construct," that biology does mean something for the way that men and women act in relation to each other and their children? Or what if you think that power is not unequally distributed among men and women? For that matter, what if you don't believe that it is the job of a professor to free your students from "nationalism"? These various departments at institutions both large and small, with students both elite and average, are advertising their lack of a need for academic freedom.

At the other end of the political spectrum are a few schools that offer courses with clear political agendas. Patrick Henry College in Purcelville, Virginia, for example, is an evangelical college mostly geared toward children from homeschool backgrounds. The school purports to be a sort of political training ground for young conservatives headed into fields like government service. A cursory glance at the school's website would suggest that professors do not have much wiggle room at all when it comes to asking big questions of their students. But then Patrick Henry doesn't offer tenure. If a school's goal is to be a political boot camp of sorts, there is little reason to allow for much inquiry or protection for those who deviate from the party line.

Many universities want to play host to disciplines in which almost no "inquiry" is actually required. That's fine. But these departments should not be able to sail under false colors either. They needn't deceive themselves or the public by claiming the protections of academic freedom.

If you count faculty in vocationally oriented departments, those who teach area, ethnic, cultural, and gender studies, as well as a significant chunk of the country's research scientists, you will arrive at a number that is more than half the tenured faculty in the United States.

At the very least, there is no reason why tenure shouldn't be abolished at the vast majority of the four thousand degree-granting colleges and universities in the United States where academic freedom is an almost irrelevant concept. When professors are engaged in imparting basic literacy skills, or even classes on how to cook or how to start a business, there is no reason why their academic freedom must be protected. At that point professors are just like any other employee. They have the right to speak freely, as guaranteed by the Constitution, but they don't have the right to say whatever they want in their role at the university. And they don't have a right to a job regardless of what sort of nonsense they spout publicly.

Administrators, faculty, and parents may disagree about which disciplines are vocational, which ones have "pre-stipulated" political goals, and which professors have already sold their academic freedom to the highest bidder. The goal of this chapter is not to make determinations about each faculty member or department. It is rather to suggest that the burden of proof should be on professors. They should have to show parents and taxpayers that there is some reason why academic freedom is necessary for them to do the job they have taken on.

*"It's publish or perish, and he hasn't published."*

# 3

# Stop the Academic Presses: Get Teachers Back in the Classroom

Elliott West didn't seem like the coolest guy on campus when I met him in the fall of 2009. With his tweed coat and thinning hair, he appeared to be the stereotype of a studious professor, only truly at home among library stacks or in a dusty archive. But West, who teaches American history at the University of Arkansas, was in the midst of a heated public competition: he was one of three finalists in a contest that confers a prize on the best college teacher in America. In the highest sense of the word, West is a competitive performer.

The prize itself—sponsored by Baylor University and called the Cherry Teaching Award, after the late alumnus whose donation made it possible—is one of the biggest money awards that an American professor can win ($200,000). And its measure of merit is not scholarly output but classroom performance—that crucial aspect of the teaching mission that is so often overshadowed, these days, by the arcana of specialized research and the mad race for publication and tenure.

The Cherry Award seeks out college teachers who, according to both students and fellow teachers, are especially good at making clear, forceful, inspiring, knowledge-rich classroom presentations that actually help students learn. The finalists for the 2009–2010 year included, in addition to West, Roger Rosenblatt of Stony Brook and Edward Burger of Williams College. Each was asked to deliver a public lecture at Baylor and another lecture on his home campus. The winner—chosen by a panel of Baylor-appointed judges—will have the privilege of spending a semester teaching at Baylor (as well as cashing that hefty award check).

On an unseasonably warm fall day at the University of Arkansas in Fayetteville, hundreds of West's students and colleagues, along with interested observers, crowded into a standing-room-only lecture hall to hear him talk about "The West Before Lewis and Clark." Over the course of forty-five minutes he spun stories of three individuals living beyond the Mississippi in the century before the great explorers set out. The Frenchman, the Spanish woman, and the Osage Indian were, he said, meant to illustrate how the West was the setting for an "imperial tussle."

West is not a comedian. There were occasional moments of levity, as when he cited an article about the Frenchman, who, at the age of fifteen, murdered his ship's captain: "Precocious depravity," West said with a chuckle. A PowerPoint presentation was running behind him, but it was a series of old maps and photographs. No words were flying around the screen. There was no audience participation, and there were no props either. Professor West does not go in for theatrics. But the people filling the seats were rapt. No one around me whispered or even checked his iPhone.

Over lunch, West tells me that "every teacher needs to find his style" and that his is "old-fashioned lecturing." He observes that he has become more "conversational" over forty years of teaching; not once during his lecture did he consult any notes. Professors, he says, need to figure out how to play to their strengths—by listening and watching their students carefully. "I look out at every class to figure out what's working and what's not." In other words, while he could be coasting at this point in his career, giving the same worn-out lectures and barely glancing at his students' reactions, he still works pretty hard. And he makes his students work pretty hard too.

Tricks and devices can help make a good teacher, he says. For instance, "Never underestimate the power of dead air." West advises "asking a question and simply waiting for the answer." He has noticed that "people will get very uncomfortable and start squirming, until someone will try." For the really tough crowds, he says, he will surprise them. They think he is carrying around a cup of coffee, but actually he has candy inside the cup. When someone finally answers a question correctly, he will throw a piece to that student. He smiles slyly: "It's like training seals."

Edward Burger is not Elliott West's polar opposite, but Burger, a professor of mathematics at Williams College and another finalist for the Cherry Award, is a magnetic personality. When we walked into a restaurant in Williamstown, Massachusetts, on a Friday night, he was the most popular guy in the room. Freshmen kept coming over to introduce him to their families, who were in town for first-year parents' weekend.

At a lecture on Saturday morning, hundreds of families packed the hall to hear Burger—a featured attraction of parents' weekend—talk about, well, math. The audience was rolling in the aisles as he proved, mathematically, that an infinite number of monkeys at an infinite number of typewriters could produce *Hamlet*.

Like West, Burger believes that empathy is the key to good teaching. Whether he is teaching a seminar at Williams or a class of two hundred at the University of Colorado, where he has been a visiting professor, Burger says he wants "to think about what it's like to be sitting in that audience, in a sea of people, when the professor is so far away he's a dot and I'm looking at overhead transparencies. What is that experience like?"

Burger suggests that the role of a teacher is to change lives. His own path was changed as an undergraduate. He planned to be a lawyer, but the math professors at Connecticut College "just kept feeding coal into the fire." And so he went to graduate school "to find out what math really is." He never got to law school.

As much as he finds math fascinating, he realizes that most people will not use calculus after college. The utilitarian promise "is an empty one," he notes. "You don't need to know how to build a bridge to go over one." He says that the hardest thing professors can ask themselves is "the ten-year question—What will my students retain from my class ten years out?" His lecture was devoted to showing the audience how to "think mathematically."

Burger, who acknowledges being one of the tougher graders on campus—"I don't give grades; I just report the news"—said he is convinced a student understands a concept only when he can "explain it to an eight-year-old." I wouldn't put it past him to bring a fourth grader to class for that purpose, but he says he just forces students to explain concepts without using jargon.

Despite his popularity, Burger confesses to me that he sometimes feels too old to be teaching, that the profession is a "young man's game." And he worries about how he will continue to communicate well with students a few years from now.

Roger Rosenblatt, the Cherry Award's third finalist, has always had to get across his ideas without jargon. As a former commentator for the *NewsHour* on PBS, he has had to address, routinely, a larger and more general audience than either West or Burger. The lecture he gave at Baylor, on "why we tell stories," was relaxed and entertaining. But not too entertaining. "You can be entertaining at the expense of being useful," he tells me. "At the end of the class, they think, 'Wasn't he delightful?' But they don't learn anything."

Like the other finalists, Professor Rosenblatt says it took him a while to develop a style. But the most important thing young professors can do, he says, is "learn their subject well. Otherwise it's just chatter."

The best professors he had in school, Rosenblatt recalls, "worried about their subjects in front of us," almost as if they were thinking aloud. "When I saw a teacher lost in thought in front of me, I knew I had the goods." He mentions one in particular, John Kelleher, the late professor of Irish studies at Harvard. "I hadn't the slightest idea about Irish studies," Rosenblatt says, but "I was smart enough to know that Kelleher was the man I wanted to study with." It was "the seriousness with which Kelleher took learning and the seriousness with which he took students that was a model to me."

All three finalists for the Cherry Award emphasize that teaching is something you have to work at. It takes time to prepare. It takes time to practice. It takes time to process the feedback from students. It takes time to grade papers and exams in a manner that is helpful. Maybe all that sounds obvious, but the truth is that many professors don't bother. It's an old observation but a true one. At most colleges, promotion and tenure decisions are made based on a record of publication.

The research bears this out: "In 1998–1999, for the vast majority of faculty irrespective of institutional type, teaching an additional hour remained a negative factor in pay and publishing an extra article a positive factor in pay." That's right. According to a 2005 article by James Fairweather in the *Journal of Higher Education, college professors actually get paid less the more time they spend in a classroom.* This is true not only at large research universities but at small liberal arts colleges, whose primary mission is to educate undergraduates.

The complaint that professors spend excessive amounts of time on scholarly publication instead of focusing their efforts in the classroom is not a new one. In 1968 Christopher Jencks and David Riesman ended their exhaustive survey of higher education, *The Academic Revolution,* with a section on "the art of teaching." Professors, they noted, "have only a limited amount of time and energy, and they know that in terms of professional standing and personal advancement it makes more sense to throw this into research than teaching."

Doug Bennett, president of Earlham College in Indiana, recalls his days teaching at Temple University. "Every faculty member I worked with at Temple would have a Monday, Wednesday, Friday schedule or a Tuesday, Thursday schedule. They would work hard to come to campus as little as possible on other days so they could do research and write. They weren't available to their students."

In the decades that followed Riesman and Jencks's observations, faculty members threw even more of their time into research. As Mark Bauerlein recently wrote in a paper for the American Enterprise Institute, "Professors on the Production Line, Students on Their Own," over the past five decades the number of language and literature publications has risen from thirteen thousand to seventy-two thousand while the audience for such scholarship "has diminished, with unit sales for books now hovering around 300." Ohio University economist Richard Vedder estimates that about two million academic articles are published each year.

Roger Baldwin, author of *Tenure on Trial: Case Studies of Change in Faculty Employment Policies*, recalls that when he began his career at the College of William and Mary in 1984, people would "assemble materials to be considered by a tenure committee in two three-ring binders. By the time I left in 2001, people were delivering it in multiple Xerox boxes." When it came to publication, he says, "expectations had been ratcheted up." Baldwin, who is now an education professor at Michigan State University, believes that the relationship between tenure and publication "is not a completely healthy thing."

The institution of tenure has long been at the center of this teaching-research problem in two ways. First, to get tenure, professors must publish. "Tenure is largely about showing that you are a research scholar, not a superb teacher," says Carol Schneider, president of the Association of American Colleges and Universities. This is "not a design [she] would have invented." And its problems are manifold: tenure, she says, has led to "a whole set of unintended consequences, including a distortion of faculty roles."

Which brings us to the second problem. Many senior faculty would prefer to engage in research and publication, and teach as little as possible. They believe that the role of professors is to contribute to a

body of literature in their disciplines, not to instruct untutored undergraduates about it. The job security offered by the institution of
tenure allows professors to skimp on their teaching responsibilities
and concentrate their attention on research. At the highest level of the
profession, faculty are lured to elite universities by promises of few or
no hours at all in the classroom.

These problems have been exacerbated in recent years as subsidies
for research have grown. The dollars come from universities themselves,
which are now engaged in national and global competition for the prestige that comes from plenty of scholarly publication. In 2007 federal
research grants to universities and related institutions came to more
than $32 billion, according to the *Statistical Abstract of the United States.*
State governments and private firms, like pharmaceutical companies,
add billions more.

Mark Schneider, a former commissioner of the U.S. Department of
Education's National Center for Education Statistics, points out that at
most public research universities the contractual teaching load is "4-4,"
that is, four courses in each of two semesters every year. But most faculty members at these institutions actually teach "2-2." In other words,
they are ostensibly spending half their time doing research.

What's behind this arrangement? As Schneider explains, "The state
is saying, 'We're in the knowledge production industry, not just the
teaching industry. So we're going to subsidize the research enterprise by
giving people reduced teaching loads.'" A former department chair at
Stony Brook, Schneider got to see firsthand how few faculty members
were actually fulfilling their research requirements. He even tried to get
the members of his department who weren't producing to teach more
classes—with little success, he laments. And he can't help but wonder
whether the professors who are publishing really deserve the amount
of the subsidy they receive. Given how long it takes the average faculty
member to produce an article, Schneider estimates that it costs the state
about $50,000 per article.

"You can make a pretty good case," says Richard Vedder, "that most of the research done to earn tenure is darn near useless. On any rational cost-benefit basis, the institution of tenure has led to the publication of hundreds of thousands of papers that are useless and read by a dozen people."

Which raises an important question, perhaps the *most* important question for parents, students, and colleges: What is the aim of higher education in the United States? The chasm is growing between where parents and taxpayers believe their education dollars are going and where they actually end up. According to a 2004 *Chronicle of Higher Education* survey, 71 percent of Americans thought it was very important to prepare undergraduate students for a career, whereas 56 percent of them thought it was very important for colleges to "discover more about the world through research." The survey doesn't specify what kind of research, though most people outside the ivory tower might assume that a pollster meant scientific research, not humanities or social science research.

One indication of the worth people place on social science research can be garnered from this survey finding: only 35 percent of respondents felt it was very important for colleges to "provide useful information to the public on issues affecting their daily lives." (Imagine what they might think about research on information that *wasn't* useful.) Faculty's understanding of their role—as experts who will advise the government and the public about the important issues of the day—does not necessarily fit with the public's understanding of faculty.

As Rick Hess of the American Enterprise Institute notes, "State legislators and parents and students see the core business of state universities as undergraduate education." But that's not what the faculty see. To the extent the professors are interested in teaching at all, Hess says, "the faculty who wind up at these institutions think of graduate seminars as the most fruitful kind of teaching." Mostly, though, professors "are hired for their research acumen and trained as researchers."

In 1990 Ernest Boyer, a former U.S. commissioner of education and former chancellor of the State University of New York, was tiring of the overemphasis on research and published a report called "Scholarship Reconsidered." He argued that the definition of scholarship should be expanded to include four categories: discovery, integration, application, and teaching. Not only, he argued, should publication be more closely connected with the teaching enterprise, but the two should also be considered of equal importance on the university campus.

Under this new model, the ideal professor is one who is both an active researcher *and* a devoted teacher. That there has always been a connection between the two is taken for granted. Riesman and Jencks wrote, "Teachers cannot remain stimulating unless they also continue to learn, and while this learning may not focus on small, manageable 'research problems,' it is research by any reasonable definition. When a teacher stops doing it, he begins to repeat himself and eventually loses touch with both the young and the world around him." Today the notion that teaching and research are mutually reinforcing activities of the "complete faculty member" has become a common talking point among academics and administrators of all stripes.

Stephan Thernstrom, an emeritus professor of history at Harvard, says that while he believes that "a lot of so-called academic research is pretty junky," he nevertheless thinks it is important for professors to continue doing research in order to be effective teachers. Thernstrom recalls a friend from graduate school who went to teach at Amherst College and didn't publish anything after his dissertation: "In some ways I think he would have been intellectually sharper and better off if he were at some place where they expected him to do research that would have been read by other experts." Thernstrom worries that there is nothing "intellectually challenging" in simply trying "to impress your undergrads." "You just have to be entertaining," he says.

One of Thernstrom's Harvard colleagues, government professor Harvey Mansfield, points out that publication requirements for tenure and promotion can ensure that a professor is not just blowing hot air at students. He explains, "There might be something of a case for publication because you do have to sit down and put something together coherently, systematically. Whereas if you find out that you're very good on your feet and know the right buttons to push for students, you can make your way as a kind of faker."

This is not to say that much of the research produced by academics is either coherent or systematic. Many journal articles read like a certain kind of fakery, as New York University professor Alan Sokal showed with his famous "hoax" article in 1996.

Sokal, a physics professor, wanted to test his belief that the intellectual standards at academic journals were dreadful. So he sent an article, "Transgressing the Boundaries: Toward a Transformative Hermeneutics of Quantum Gravity," to the journal *Social Text*. In the article he suggested that quantum gravity was really a social construct: "In quantum gravity, as we shall see, the space-time manifold ceases to exist as an objective physical reality; geometry becomes relational and contextual; and the foundational conceptual categories of prior science—among them, existence itself—become problematized and relativized. This conceptual revolution, I will argue, has profound implications for the content of a future postmodern and liberatory science."

Sprinkling his prose with the cutting-edge academic jargon of the time, Sokal wondered, "Would a leading North American journal of cultural studies . . . publish an article liberally salted with nonsense if (a) it sounded good and (b) it flattered the editors' ideological preconceptions?" The answer, he found, was yes.

But let's suppose for a minute that most of the academic research out there is decent. Does it really trickle down to the student experience as Ernest Boyer would hope? Boyer's work on the intertwining of teaching and research was unquestionably influential. Dozens of universities, both private and public, now have centers on campus devoted to improving the pedagogical practices of their faculty and integrating them with research. The National Science Foundation even requires its grantees to show how their research will improve teaching and learning.

But does this really happen? How valuable is a professor's engagement in research when it comes to teaching? And how much is teaching really valued on campus? James Fairweather asks in his paper on faculty salaries: has the "decade-long push for greater commitment to teaching and learning and to restore the balance between teaching and research [been] reflected in a key reward—faculty pay?" The answer, he found, is no. However well intentioned the administrators and faculty who have tried to bring the "scholarship of teaching and learning" to their campuses, the effects have been minimal at best. Ultimately, faculty are rational economic beings, and they will respond to incentives of pay and promotion for research, no matter how much lip service is paid to the importance of teaching.

Up and down the chain of university command, it is clear what sort of behavior is rewarded. In a recent survey of political science department chairs done by Miami University in Ohio's John Rothgeb and Betsy Burger, fewer than half the respondents at bachelor's-degree-awarding institutions (that is, those specifically devoted to undergraduate education) reported that teaching was the most important factor in deciding whether a professor would receive tenure. Forty-two percent of respondents felt that research was more important, that research and teaching were equally important, or that research, teaching, and service (on administrative committees) were all valued equally in the quest for tenure.

Administrators and faculty like to paper over this problem of priorities by suggesting that faculty don't really have to choose—the better you are at research, the better you are at teaching. But the notion that faculty members can do it all is just pie in the sky. Whatever the beliefs of administrators and faculty, there is little evidence that teaching and research are mutually reinforcing activities. In a 1996 article in the *Review of Educational Research*, John Hattie of the University of North

Carolina at Greensboro and H. W. Marsh of the University of Western
Sydney reported the results from a study of fifty-eight institutions. They
could not find any relationship at all between research productivity and
teaching effectiveness.

For the most part, teaching and research are separate activities
competing for a faculty member's time. It is little wonder, then, that
Fairweather found "the complete faculty member" to be a "rarity." "For
most faculty members," he wrote in a 2002 paper for the *Journal of
Higher Education*, "generating high numbers of student contact hours
diminishes publication rates, and vice versa."

There is no question that tenure encourages an overabundance of
publishing. And this publishing does little for the undergraduate student who is competing for a professor's time. The problem is not just
the quantity of publication, though, it's the type of publication—and
what the rate and type of publication have done to academic disciplines,
the university, and the student body over time.

Let's return for a moment to the idea of the German model of a
research university discussed in the preceding chapter. It was, as American progressives like John Dewey envisioned it, always supposed to be
breaking new ground. Dewey worried that the traditional university
education consisted of "to a large extent the cultural products of societ-
ies that assumed the future would be much like the past." But, of course,
the future would be different.

The idea that universities must always be changing, that they need
to be on the cutting edge, began in America with the progressives but
has become a fairly common trope in the rest of society too. At a conference on the "Campus of the Future" a few years ago, administrators
from around the country gathered in Honolulu to learn how higher
education would need to change if it was to set the pace for the modern
world. According to an account from the *Chronicle of Higher Education*,

keynote speaker Thomas Friedman "urged educators to focus less on concrete outcomes like grades and test scores and more on teaching students how to learn, instilling passion and curiosity in them and developing their intuitive skills." The *New York Times* columnist suggested to his audience of four thousand that preparing students for an uncertain future was akin to "training for the Olympics without knowing which sport you will compete in."

This blustery overstatement is also painfully familiar: change is so rapid, we are told, that we can't even imagine what education in the future will look like. I recently found myself at a "career night" at my old high school where I heard ideas similar to Friedman's. An alumnus on my panel advised students that "the job [you] will hold probably doesn't even exist today."

One has to wonder whether such claims will become, for students and teachers, an excuse for laziness. Remember the young Alvy Singer in Woody Allen's *Annie Hall?* Upon finding out that the universe will eventually come to an end, he decides to stop doing his homework. In similar fashion, students today, who are hectored about the hyperchanging world they live in, and professors, who are always looking for the next new thing coming down the pike, may decide that there is no point in traditional learning since the future will be so very different.

Professors, even in the humanities, have constantly had to show that they too could be breaking new ground, so much so that they have left that old-time knowledge behind. As Patrick Deneen, professor of political science at Georgetown University, explains, they must "prove their worth in the eyes of administrators in the broader world. Faculty could demonstrate their progressiveness by showing the backwardness of texts; they could 'create knowledge' by demonstrating their own superiority to the authors they studied; they could demonstrate their anti-traditionalism by attacking the very books that were the basis of their discipline."

As if all this novelty weren't enough, they also must write it in a sort of code. Deneen says, "By adopting a jargon only comprehensible to a few 'experts' they could emulate the priesthood of scientists—wholly betraying the original mandate of the humanities to guide students through the cultural inheritance and teachings of the classic books." Critics, and especially journalists, like to joke about how the prose of academics is largely unreadable. This is not an accident. The jargon is a signal to other academics that they are "experts." The more unreadable the prose, the more successful professors count themselves. And it's gotten worse in recent years. Pick up an academic book from the 1960s and it's almost guaranteed to be more understandable than one written in the 1990s.

Moreover, professors no longer receive "credit" for publishing works in nonacademic journals. Claire Potter, a history professor at Wesleyan, says she wishes more assistant professors were "writing book reviews for the *Wall Street Journal.*" They don't, she says, "because it doesn't count" in the small world of people who determine whether or not they get tenure. A book review in a major newspaper probably won't be breaking new scholarly ground, but that doesn't mean it's not contributing in some way to knowledge of the field. In fact it's spreading that knowledge to people who might not otherwise get it. Whether they're educated readers or striving undergraduates, they're worth reaching.

Professors today are not what Deneen would call "guides" passing on an "inheritance." They are always and everywhere trying to say something novel. But is this an activity that best serves their students, particularly their undergraduates? Mark Bauerlein accurately describes academic publishing as "an economy focused not on the commodity or the consumer, but on the producer alone." The professor does not submit himself humbly to the needs of students or institutions or even ideas. He is the center of his universe.

Bauerlein notes, "As opposed to physical sciences where advancing discoveries and technologies create new domains of inquiry, the primary materials of language and literature don't much change." He acknowledges that there are a few contemporary authors to be analyzed but observes that "their addition doesn't nearly account for the swelling critical publication."

In 2008, according to the *Year's Work in English Literature,* more than one hundred new scholarly books were published on Shakespeare. What were the authors thinking? First, no doubt, of tenure.

Tenure depends on the professor's ability to say something new, but it is no longer easy to carve out new things to say. That may be one of the reasons it takes so long to get through graduate school these days— *an average of eleven years to get a doctorate in English.* As Louis Menand wrote in a 2009 article for *Harvard Magazine,* "That it takes longer to get a PhD in the humanities than it does in the social or natural sciences . . . seems anomalous, since normally a dissertation in the humanities does not require extensive archival, field or laboratory work." One reason, he offers, is that "people are uncertain just what research in the humanities is supposed to constitute, and graduate students therefore spend an inordinate amount of time trying to come up with a novel theoretical twist on canonical texts or an unusual contextualization." It's exhausting just thinking about it. With thousands of PhDs being minted every year, topics are drying up by the minute.

Such a system produces needless obstacles for those in the academic pipeline. After all, wouldn't a person, educated broadly within his or her discipline, be qualified to teach most undergraduate courses? Wouldn't someone who has spent more time on that broad education and less time trying to find some miniscule niche of a topic on which to write a dissertation be the better teacher for most of those classes?

And forget about the idea of having a professor who understands multiple disciplines and can explain their relation to one another. As David Perlmutter, the *Chronicle of Higher Education's* career advice columnist, explains, "Tenure candidates who explore multiple research topics are perceived as 'unfocused.' They don't establish a 'clear trajectory' or 'delineate a tight subspecialization.'" He concludes mockingly, "Preach interdisciplinarity; build the silos higher."

The problem is not just publishing in order to get tenure. Carlin Romano, critic at large for the *Chronicle of Higher Education*, notes that sometimes "getting tenure creates the feeling of liberation that drives scholars into areas in which they have no expertise or into trivial subjects or hobby horses no one else cares about." In 2000, for instance, Harvard English professor Elaine Scarry took a break from literary criticism to write extensively on her theory that the crash of TWA Flight 800 off the coast of Long Island was caused by electromagnetic interference from military ships and planes. Even if parents paying tuition believe that faculty need to engage in research in order to remain good teachers, this is probably not what they had in mind.

The growing emphasis on research has also produced a harmful effect on the disciplines themselves, trickling down even to the popularity of certain majors among undergraduates. The fact that graduate students and faculty members are forced to go farther and farther afield in order to find something new to say in the discipline makes the discipline itself less coherent.

In a 2009 article in the *American Scholar*, William Chace, former president of Wesleyan and an emeritus professor of English at Emory, notes that "in one generation" (from 1970 to 2003) the numbers of undergraduates majoring in the humanities dropped from 30 percent to less than 16 percent. He blames the decline on the "failure of English departments across the country to champion, with passion, the books they teach and to make a strong case to undergraduates that the knowledge of those books and the tradition in which they exist is a human good in and of itself."

Chace continues, with a passion of his own, "What departments have done instead is dismember the curriculum, drift away from the notion that historical chronology is important, and substitute for the books themselves a scattered array of secondary considerations (identity

studies, abstruse theory, sexuality, film and popular culture)." He cites
the Harvard English department, which recently replaced its year-long
survey course for English majors with a series of "affinity groups" in
which students learn about whatever authors (within broad categories
like "poets") their particular professor finds important or interesting.
Chace points out that under this system the job of "cobbling together
intellectual coherence" falls to the students themselves.

In fact, if you read enough college viewbooks and websites, you get
the sense that administrators see this state of affairs as an asset to their
campuses. The college catalog has become a kind of choose-your-own-
adventure book. It sounds intellectually exciting, but for an eighteen-
year-old to map a coherent path of, say, thirty-two courses out of the
hundreds (if not thousands) listed is plainly unreasonable.

To reform this situation in which faculty members overspecialize
and students are left twisting in the wind, Chace suggests redefining
the standards for tenure. He wants to place "more emphasis on the
classroom and less on published research." And he says that his fellow English professors "should prepare to contest our decisions with
administrators whose science-based model is not an appropriate means
for evaluation." He continues, "Released from the obligation to deliver
research results in the form of little-read monographs and articles, hu-
manists could then resolve to spend their time teaching what they love
to students glad to learn."

Chace makes a good point. What if we just changed the standards for
tenure? Wouldn't that solve the problem of too much bad research and
too little quality teaching? Tenure is typically granted for research that
has already been completed. But teaching is in need of constant evaluation. Of course, there is reason to believe that professors who have been
good researchers in the past will continue to be so, and that those who
have been good teachers in the past will continue to be so. But that's not

always the case. Even the best professors, like Edward Burger, wonder whether they will still be as good in the decades to come. Why not help them with the kind of consistent performance evaluations that usually disappear once tenure is granted (if they were ever conducted at all)?

Some professors may simply tire of putting the effort into teaching. And for them, the incentives built into a tenure system are all wrong. Tenure means they can simply neglect their students with little or no consequence. In fact, the incentives provided by tenure are not right for any school that wants to encourage better teaching.

A professor who has been awarded tenure because of brilliant research is still considered an asset to the university even if he doesn't publish a paper for the rest of his career. His reputation will draw more students, more alumni donations, more grant money, and a higher *U.S. News* ranking, as we shall see. But a professor who is awarded tenure on the basis of teaching is of no use if she decides not to put much effort into teaching any more. So why not award tenure to the publishing professor? With his prestigious award or peer-reviewed article, he is a sure bet—at least in some sense.

A few universities are beginning to push back against this trend by hiring "professors of practice." These are faculty members who are hired for their teaching acumen. Instead of tenure, they are typically awarded multi-year contracts.

As Peter Lange, the provost of Duke University told me, "The structure of the tenure system was ill adapted to bringing that quality of teaching to campus, to bringing in teaching faculty in a way that gave the person status and possibility for promotion based on what they did well." These professors of practice now constitute 16 percent of Duke's arts and sciences faculty, according to Lange. They are typically awarded three-to-five-year contracts to start and have salaries that are commensurate with those of their colleagues on the tenure track. It is a model that other schools are looking at.

For most schools, though, the completely lopsided emphasis on research is only growing worse. Eugene Rice, director of the Forum on Faculty Roles and Rewards at the American Association of Higher Education, says that the "prestige economy drives faculty." Which doesn't sound like a bad thing in and of itself. Shouldn't we want schools to compete with one another? Won't these contests ultimately improve performance?

In principle, yes. But this works only if schools are competing against other schools with similar goals and similar students. Gary Rhoades, general secretary of the American Association of University Professors, tells of an acquaintance who teaches at an institution in Colorado and who recently met the school's new provost. According to the acquaintance, the provost said, "We're going to be the Harvard of the Platt River Valley." Perhaps apocryphal, the story does illustrate a certain truth that some administrators miss. First, it's not going to happen, and second, as Rhoades correctly asks, "Why would you want it to happen? The Platt River Valley doesn't need a Harvard. It needs something else."

But most ranking systems, *U.S. News* being the most prominent, have created the illusion of a ladder that every school, from the regional community college to the elite university, can climb, if only they can game the numbers correctly. The formula for determining the *U.S. News* ranking of a school is complex and varies slightly from year to year. But parents should make an effort to understand it before they rely on it.

Certain factors have always been well rewarded by *U.S. News.* They include the salary of faculty and the school's overall reputation in the eyes of its peers. *U.S. News* sends administrators a survey asking about schools in the same general category as their own. While some have routinely given poor grades to other institutions in order to boost their own rankings—a couple of years ago, the provost at the University of Wisconsin at Madison, for instance, determined that 260 of its 262 peer institutions were of merely "adequate" quality—most base their conclusions on the level of prestige an institution has achieved. In this regard, provosts and presidents at other schools may have some sense of the level of publication of faculty members at other institutions. But they would have no way of knowing about the quality of the teaching there.

In 2010 the *U.S. News* editors responded to criticism of their "peer review" formula by asking high school guidance counselors to weigh in on the reputations of various colleges as well. These counselors may provide a different perspective, but their opinions still are not likely to be informed by the quality of teaching on campus.

As Alexander McCormick explains, "Teaching doesn't have a mechanism for recognition beyond the borders of campus." McCormick is director of the National Survey of Student Engagement (NSSE), an instrument that was developed ten years ago, in part as a response to the excesses of *U.S. News.* NSSE measures issues like how much time students spend in class or doing their homework, how often they ask questions in class, and other factors that bear on a student's actual campus experience.

McCormick and others say that it may be more difficult but not impossible to measure teachers beyond the borders of campus. On a small scale, this is what the Cherry Teaching Awards are aiming at. They are not ranking every teacher at every institution; they are providing a way for faculty to be recognized beyond the borders of their campus for their teaching abilities.

Moreover the Cherry Awards also suggest that there are ways to measure the quality of teaching. Somehow, students from around the country and committee members they never met managed to produce a list of people that almost everyone would agree are very talented teachers.

In his recent book *Crisis on Campus*, Mark Taylor proposes the creation of a National Teaching Academy to elevate the status of teaching across the country. It would be "sponsored jointly by the federal government, individual private donations, corporations, and leading colleges and universities throughout the country." Taylor suggests that the "academy's primary mission would be to support outstanding professors who would be appointed to develop high-quality seminars, classes, and other programs for faculty members from educational institutions that do not have the resources to underwrite proper and continuing faculty development." Taylor, a veteran educator at both a small college (Williams) and a large university (Columbia), seems confident that the quality of teaching is measurable and universally recognizable.

Many faculty members have suggested to me that good teaching is just something you know when you see it. But David Caputo, president emeritus at Pace University in New York, says that answer is a cop-out. He is sure that the assessment of teaching is "*not* like the Supreme Court's definition of obscenity." It is possible to determine how good a teacher is, "but it takes an investment of time and money." And it also takes a commitment from people at the top of the institution to be interested in questions of teaching.

John Silber, the former long-time president of Boston University, told me that he never gave professors tenure without sitting in on their classes first. The idea of a university president hanging out in the back of a classroom is almost unheard of. But Silber insists that it is easy to tell a good teacher from a bad one: "I damn sure wouldn't hire or promote a faculty member to anything like that salary without having known what they are doing [in the classroom]."

Even some faculty will acknowledge that an administrator is perfectly capable of determining whether a professor is a good teacher or not. Lorne Carmichael, an economist at Queens University in Canada, defends the institution of tenure but thinks it is important mostly for research professors, not teachers: "An administrator is probably quite capable in a classroom of figuring out who is doing well," he tells me. The only reason to have faculty evaluating one another's work and granting tenure is because the research is so narrow (and, in some cases, advanced) that only other people in the field can possibly understand it. Good teaching should be recognizable to anyone who can put himself in the mind-set of a college freshman.

John Silber didn't mind making enemies on the Boston University campus, and he had a reputation for, to put it mildly, a top-down management approach, which many faculty didn't appreciate. But they don't like the bottom-up approach either. Try saying the words "student evaluations" to a room filled with academics and you will be booed and hissed out of the lecture hall.

It is true that student evaluations are inexact. College kids can be immature, and the evaluation forms can provide a means for them to act on their petty grudges. Ron Ehrenberg, an economics professor at Cornell, says he has seen how professors can improve their evaluations—by making lectures more entertaining, using jokes or a different tone of voice. Professors will score higher, but experiments show that the students haven't learned anything more.

A recent program implemented at the University of Texas, in which faculty who receive positive student evaluations earn bonuses of up to $10,000, may encourage much kowtowing to students. Faculty will likely elevate student grades and/or simplify the material they teach. Reliance on student evaluations as the sole measure of job performance is not the key to improving teaching quality.

As Stanley Fish wrote in his blog on the *New York Times* website in response to the news about Texas evaluations: "If a waiter asks me, 'Was everything to your taste, sir?', I am in a position to answer him authoritatively (if I choose to). When I pick up my shirt from the dry cleaner, I immediately know whether the offending spot has been removed. But when, as a student, I exit from a class or even from an entire course, it may be years before I know whether I got my money's worth, and that goes both ways. A course I absolutely loved may turn out be worthless because the instructor substituted wit and showmanship for an explanation of basic concepts. And a course that left me feeling confused and convinced I had learned very little might turn out to have planted seeds that later grew into mighty trees of understanding. 'Deferred judgment' or 'judgment in the fullness of time' seems to be appropriate to the evaluation of teaching."

Most observers say that student evaluations do contain *some* important information. They can tell you who the best teachers are and who the worst ones are, according to Mark Schneider of the American Enterprise Institute. It's the ones in the middle that are harder to evaluate. But there are ways to improve the kind of information that one receives from such evaluations.

Doug Bennett, president of Earlham College (a school of eleven hundred students in rural Indiana) says that his school's evaluations are not filled with multiple-choice questions. "We ask students to tell us what is going on in the classroom. We ask them to write sentences," Bennett says. (Earlham also has faculty members sitting in on one another's classes every semester.)

Certainly this is a good start, but what are students actually learning from these faculty members? Surveys like the Collegiate Learning Assessment try to determine how much knowledge a student has acquired from all their professors during all their years of school. Others, like NSSE, try to determine how much contact students have with their professors. But none of these measure the quality of the teacher based on how much students are learning from him or her on an individual level.

In evaluating teaching, it's obviously important to have student input because the kids are the ones most often in the class. But they are also the ones who are least likely to know (at that age, anyway) what will be most useful to them in their careers and in their adult lives generally. There is a way to get around this. Mark Schneider suggests that schools should be able to match student records with state unemployment records. At its crudest, this system could look at students who graduated with degrees in political science from two comparable schools. If they show significant income disparities, one department or group of professors might be the problem. This measurement might yield some interesting results, or it might not. But we need to think about new ways of evaluating the quality of teaching.

A more nuanced approach would be for schools to survey young alumni, to ask which professors or courses they found to be most and least important or helpful in their lives after graduation, to get their "deferred judgment." This would allow students to get over any anger they had at getting a lower grade than they expected and also give them the lens of real-life experience with which to reflect on their college years.

Measuring the quality of teaching is not a fool's errand. The methods for doing so are proliferating, and it's time that colleges start paying attention. In 2008 *Forbes* magazine teamed with Richard Vedder and his staff at the Center for College Affordability and Productivity to devise a new kind of ranking. This one, Vedder said, would be based on "outcomes," not inputs. Whereas *U.S. News*, for instance, might measure the SATs of a high school student entering a school, the *Forbes* survey would measure a student's salary coming out. Whereas *U.S. News* might place more weight on the salary of faculty, Vedder's survey would look at the number of awards (like Rhodes scholarships) that students receive. A whopping 25 percent of the *Forbes* ranking was based on student satisfaction with course instruction. The researchers also evaluated schools based on the amount of debt students graduated with. In other words, Vedder and his team wanted to know about how much bang students were getting for their buck. Critics have suggested that Vedder's use of a website called ratemyprofessors.com has produced some statistically skewed results about student satisfaction with particular schools, but Vedder maintains that it is still a better way to cull the information he wants than the traditional alternatives.

Some of the same schools that topped the charts at *U.S. News* made the *Forbes* list as well—Harvard, Princeton, Yale, Williams, and Amherst all placed in the top ten. But the number 1 slot was occupied by West Point and the fourteenth place by Centre College, a small school in Kentucky. Whitman College in Washington State made number 20. And Wabash in Ohio was number 32.

The *Forbes* ranking may not be for everyone, but it does give aspiring undergraduates a more reasonable projection of what they, as students, can expect from a variety of colleges and universities, both public and private, across the country.

The American Council of Trustees and Alumni also launched a new survey in 2009. "What Will They Learn" rates each school on whether it requires seven core subjects: composition, literature, foreign language, U.S. government or history, economics, mathematics, and natural or physical science. Using the school's course catalog, the researchers at ACTA investigate whether a student will have a broad base of knowledge in a variety of subjects upon graduation. For instance, here is the Council's description of its history requirement: "A survey course in either U.S. government or history, with enough chronological and topical breadth to expose students to the sweep of American history and institutions. Narrow, niche courses do not count for the requirement, nor do courses that only focus on a narrow chronological period or a specific state or region." Natural science courses must include a laboratory component. Mathematics courses count only if they involve real math, not, say, a computer literacy class. The schools that have received a grade of A from ACTA are not generally those that are at the top of the *U.S. News* list. They include Baylor University in Texas, Hunter College in New York, and the University of Arkansas.

It's probably just a coincidence that one of the finalists for the Cherry Awards, Elliott West, teaches at one of the schools given an A by ACTA. Or that another finalist, Edward Burger, is from one of the schools ranked in the top ten by *Forbes*. On the other hand, successful teaching doesn't occur in a vacuum. Universities that support strong undergraduate instruction over research and publication are likely to produce faculty who put time into teaching. The surest way to guarantee that higher education's priorities shift in the right direction is by eliminating tenure.

PART-TIME     ASSOCIATE     TENURED

# 4

# The Academic Underclass

In his 1988 novel *Nice Work*, the British academic David Lodge offers readers a telling conversation between Robyn Penrose, a postmodernist feminist English professor, and Vic Wilcox, the managing director of an iron foundry. Upon learning about the system of tenure at universities, Wilcox can hardly contain his disbelief:

> "You mean they've got jobs for life?" he said.
>
> "Well, yes. But the government wants to abolish tenure in the future."
>
> "I should think so."
>
> "But it's essential!" Robyn exclaimed. "It's the only guarantee of academic freedom. It's one of the things we were demonstrating for last week."
>
> "Hang about," said Wilcox. "You were demonstrating in support of other lecturers' right to a job for life?"
>
> "Partly," said Robyn.
>
> "But if they can't be shifted, there'll never be room for you, no matter how much better than them you may be at the job."
>
> This thought had crossed Robyn's mind before, but she had suppressed it as ignoble.

Not long after *Nice Work* was published, Margaret Thatcher reformed tenure at British universities, making it possible to dismiss faculty who were no longer deemed qualified or capable of the work for which they were hired. (Almost all the universities in the United Kingdom are public, so the prime minister had the power to accomplish this.) Lodge's novel not only illustrated what many Brits saw as the growing disconnect between the university and the rest of the economy but also exposed one of the oddest facets of the tenure system. The people on the bottom of the academic ladder are hurt by it the most, yet they have continued to support it. Tenure helps ensure that adjunct professors form the lumpenproletariat of the university system.

Nancy Jimeno didn't go to college until she was forty, but the way she talks about the academic life—her students, her discipline—you'd think she was born on a quad. Jimeno had worked in the jewelry business for all of her young adult life but decided, finally, that she wanted a professional career. She graduated summa cum laude from Cal State Fullerton in political science and then, with the encouragement of a mentor there, she began to think about graduate school. She concentrated on environmental politics and decided she would write a dissertation about land-use laws in California.

"I was very naive when I started graduate school," Jimeno tells me. "I thought as soon as I was ABD [all but dissertation completed], I would get work." She did get work, of a sort, but not the career she envisioned.

While a graduate student at Fullerton, Jimeno began working as a teaching assistant at UC Riverside, a school sixty miles from her home. She assisted with three classes, and in return her graduate school tuition was paid and she received a stipend of $700 a month. When her course work at Fullerton was done (that is, when she had no more tuition bills), she was offered a job there. The chair of the department said they could pay her $600 a month to teach her own courses as an adjunct lecturer. It was a pay cut, but Jimeno figured it would be better for her résumé if she had taught her own classes. And the commute was better too.

The job has not been easy, though. Despite having gone to Fullerton herself, Jimeno says she was surprised by the students in her class.
"Ninety percent of them," she estimates, "come from homes where English is not spoken, and 60 percent of them are not ready for college. They
need remedial work." She pauses and then adds, almost dreamily, "If I
had the time I would go over the papers with each one. I wish I could
do that. It would make such a difference in their lives. If I had the time."

She says she tries to give generous office hours, but space is limited
and it's hard to advise students when there are three other adjunct lecturers meeting with students in the same room at the same time. "Students come in with learning problems or personal problems. We have
to meet in Starbucks. I had one student who wanted to out himself to
his parents. I don't have a place for him to talk to me."

The students, she says, realize that the adjunct faculty is different:
"They know I'm not on campus most days." They also know that she
might not be around for the long term, if they should want a recommendation.

Six years after she began teaching at Fullerton, not much has changed
for Jimeno. In the fall of 2009 she received $567 per month for lead-
ing one class of sixty students. She had her own teaching assistant for
five hours a week, but three of those hours were taken up by the TA's
attendance in class. Jimeno is responsible for all the lectures and grading. In other semesters she has been paid up to $1,200 for teaching two
courses or one "supersection" of 250 students. She hasn't earned more
than $15,000 a year yet. Her daughter, she points out, "a server in a nice
restaurant," earns more than that. A starting tenure-track professor in
the department could count on at least three times that much.

Jimeno still hasn't finished her dissertation, both because of the demands of her teaching—typically twenty-five hours a week—and, she
acknowledges, because she has had to care for her ailing mother and her
granddaughter, of whom she has custody. Jimeno spends other hours
working on campus as well. She acts as faculty adviser to the Newman
Club. She has served on a committee to discuss sustainability issues at

the college, all in the hope that her prospects for advancement in the department might be improved. Instead she says she remains a "second-class citizen." Not only do tenured and tenure-track faculty have smaller classes and higher salaries, they get to choose what time they want to hold classes, Jimeno says. "They get the fun of developing new curricula. And they get to earn extra money teaching eight-week summer courses between semesters," an option not open to adjuncts.

In the time she has been there, tenure-track positions have opened up in the department, but Jimeno wasn't even granted an interview. When I spoke with her fewer than two weeks before the spring 2010 semester was to begin, she still didn't know whether she would have any courses to teach at all.

Although Jimeno says she plans to finish her dissertation, she has come to realize that she cannot stay in academia "as a career." She recalls that the chair of a politics department at another public campus in California told her that getting tenure is like winning the lottery—"you get a set amount of money every year for the rest of your life." And at age fifty-five, Jimeno figures she has about as much chance of getting a tenure-track position as she does of winning the lottery. "I know I'm good," she tells me, almost pleading her case for a teaching position. "It's the first thing in my life I've felt I have a real talent for."

Fortunately Jimeno's research has opened other doors for her. She has become active in local and state politics because of her expertise on environmental issues. Recently the *Orange County Register* called to interview her. But when they asked what her title is, she tells me, "I didn't know what to say."

Jimeno's age does not make her the typical adjunct, though adjunct faculty are on average getting older as the time to get a PhD has lengthened and the difficulty of getting a full-time tenure-track job has increased. That she is a woman and has been able to stay in academia this long only because of a spouse's salary makes her very typical, as we shall see.

Jimeno is one of hundreds of thousands of contingent faculty working in the United States today. By some estimates, faculty off the tenure track make up about 70 percent of the total and are responsible for teaching more than half of all undergraduate classes. While most adjunct faculty are concentrated at community colleges or public universities that are lower on the prestige ladder, the adjunct revolution has been growing elsewhere too.

In a book called *Off-Track Profs*, Edie Goldenberg, a former dean at the University of Michigan, Ann Arbor, and her former associate dean, John G. Cross, explore how at major research universities—including Berkeley, Cornell, Duke, Illinois, Michigan, MIT, Northwestern, Virginia, Washington, and Washington University in St. Louis—nontenure-track faculty has been growing at a rate of 3.1 percent a year since 1990, resulting in an overall increase of 36 percent.

Goldenberg says that when she became dean at Michigan she was surprised to find out how many nontenure-track faculty the school was employing. She asked Cross to get her some numbers on this phenomenon, but it turned out that "nobody knew." She recalls, "Every few weeks he was finding more lecturers." Carol Schneider, president of the American Association of Colleges and Universities, has observed this haphazard adjunct hiring on a large scale. "It's just like strip malls. It wasn't that we set out to build mile after mile of awful architecture, but we did."

Universities have always hired adjunct faculty. Sometimes they were "professionals," employed because they had a particular area of expertise: a novelist hired to teach creative writing, a lawyer hired to teach a class on constitutional law, a CPA hired to teach an accounting course. Sometimes adjuncts were brought in to deal with minor enrollment fluctuations. Suddenly more students than the department expected signed up for introductory Spanish. A local adjunct was called at the last moment to add another section of the course and meet demand.

But in more recent years administrators and department chairs have turned to adjuncts in order to save money and keep senior faculty members happy. Because adjuncts typically receive lower salaries and no benefits, are willing to teach large introductory classes that tenured faculty don't want, and are willing to sign up at the last minute, they have been a godsend for universities trying to tighten their belts. While tenured professors are fixed costs for a university, adjuncts are not. And while tenured professors can and often do decline requests by department chairs, adjuncts are so desperate for work that they rarely refuse an assignment.

Goldenberg notes that there was scarcely any concerted effort on the part of the schools she studied to hire more adjuncts—as at Michigan, the administrations were often themselves surprised at how widespread the phenomenon was. Still, there is no escaping the logic of the departments and schools that hired so many adjuncts. As Mark Bauerlein, the Emory professor and blogger for the *Chronicle of Higher Education*, told me, "The best model for administrators is adjuncts. They get no benefits; we get more kids enrolling. If you're an administrator, that's a no-brainer."

The difficulties that adjunct faculty face in trying to eke out a living have received more attention in recent years. Gene Rice, director of the Forum on Faculty Roles and Rewards at the American Association for Higher Education, says he recalls attending a professional meeting several years ago of adjuncts—"The anger in the room was really palpable." He remembers a speech by a young adjunct "piecing together a bare living without any benefits, driving up and down the freeway, with no office." Rice adds, "People literally wept."

In 1997 the documentarian Barbara Wolf chronicled the lives of these "freeway fliers" in a short film called *Degrees of Shame: Part-Time Faculty: Migrant Workers of the Information Economy.* This overwrought piece of propaganda contains interview after interview with tired-looking part-time faculty members trying to earn a meager salary from the ivory tower. One worries that his choice of career is "not fair" to his wife, who wants them to live a middle-class life. Many of the interviewees speculate about the amount of money the university is making off of them. One woman mentions the university president's limo, which she believes is paid for on the backs of adjuncts. Another man says he feels no affinity with the university's tenured faculty, who, he says, "have it made in the shade."

Perhaps the most revealing interview in the whole video, though, is with the chair of an economics and business department at an unnamed California university who describes why his department employs thirty-five to forty adjunct professors at a time. Sometimes the tenured faculty, he says, "are not available to us." Moreover, he explains that all his adjuncts could walk out in protest today and he'd be able to replace them tomorrow. "I've got a file drawer full of résumés," he says.

Even a less than astute observer of the academic labor market would wonder about this imbalance. Why does that chairman have such an abundance of people banging down his doors to take these jobs—especially if the salary and conditions are so terrible? And how can you operate a department or any kind of organization if the senior members are often simply "unavailable"?

We'll return to the second question shortly. As for the first—why so many are willing to work so hard for so little—one popular explanation is the "overproduction" of PhDs. Too many young academics competing for only a few jobs means that administrators and department chairs will always have the upper hand.

In preparation for its 2010 annual meeting, the American Historical Association released a report on the availability of jobs in the profession. It revealed that in the preceding academic year the number of help-wanted ads in the association's magazine, *Perspectives on History*, fell 23.8 percent from a year earlier, to 806 openings. Worse, 15 percent of the openings listed were later canceled.

Robert Townsend, the association's assistant director for research and publications, explained in the report, "The primary problem today, as it was a decade ago, seems to lie on the supply side of the market." He wrote that "until programs reduce the number of students . . . and revise the culture of history doctoral training, the sense of crisis in the job market for history Ph.D.s seems only likely to grow worse for the foreseeable future."

Similar sentiments have been expressed by other academic organizations, including the Modern Language Association. In 2009 a number of universities took this criticism to heart. Emory University cut its doctoral students by 40 percent—admitting 220 that fall, down from 360 a year before. Columbia reduced its intake by 10 percent. New York University also engaged in a "modest" reduction, according to officials there. And the University of South Carolina was considering a plan to have some departments admit doctoral students only every other year.

Catherine R. Stimson, dean of the Graduate School of Arts and Science at New York University, was quoted in *Inside Higher Ed*: given the state of the academic job market, she asked, referring to would-be doctoral candidates, "Is it fair to bring them in?"

It sounds like a logical question, but is it really? After all, the dire academic job market is nothing new. In a 2004 article called "Contingent Faculty and the New Academic Labor System," Gwen Bradley notes that an academic job shortage is rarely the result of some surprising lurch in supply-and-demand curves since "the same institutions both manufacture and consume the Ph.D. product." In other words, universities know very well that they are producing far more PhDs than they need. But the graduate students provide many universities with cheap labor, helping (like adjuncts) to teach large introductory classes like freshman composition.

Still, with an explosion in the number of people going to college, one might reasonably wonder why there hasn't actually been a shortage of PhDs to teach them in recent years. Two decades ago William Bowen, a former president of Princeton University, predicted as much, claiming there would soon be far more university teaching jobs than academics to fill them. He coauthored a study foreseeing "a real shortfall" in the humanities and social sciences starting in the late 1990s.

The shortage never materialized. Even during boom times there was not much of an uptick in job listings for university faculty. Any increase in job demand was met by an overwhelming increase in labor supply: universities began hiring adjunct faculty members in large numbers.

Marc Bousquet, author of *How the University Works* and a *Chronicle of Higher Education* blogger, was incredulous when he read Townsend's remarks in the AHA report. Bousquet wrote on his blog, "Most 'supply-side' solutions are doomed to fail so long as administrators have so much control over the contours of demand that they can put staff, per-matemps, and students—including undergraduates—to work at activities that were formerly done by persons holding doctorates."

So there is not an oversupply of PhDs so much as an oversupply of people willing and able (at least as far as administrators and department chairs are concerned) to perform the functions of a professor. They may or may not have completed their PhD, or even a master's degree. But they are all competing for the same positions. And maybe universities have a point. As noted earlier, the requirement that one do groundbreaking research on a narrow topic in English literature needn't be a qualification to teach freshman composition or even a survey of English literature.

Some of academia's elder statesmen have begun advising young scholars not to continue in the profession for fear they will never get decent jobs. Carol Schneider, president of the Association of American Colleges and Universities, cites a recent advice column in the *Chronicle of Higher Education* on getting a PhD: "Don't do it." She acknowledges, "That's not unlike the advice I have given people recently."

But for one reason or another, not enough people are taking this advice. The *Wall Street Journal*'s list of the two hundred best jobs in 2009 included eleven academic positions in its top fifty. The criteria included environment, income, employment outlook, physical demands, and stress. If you want to be a historian, philosopher, or anthropologist, though, you might undergo considerable stress in trying to find a job.

In 2003 a blog called *The Invisible Adjunct* launched. The author remains anonymous to this day, but in an interview with the *Chronicle* she described growing up in a working-class family in Canada. After putting herself through college, she says her advisers told her, "You're too smart for law school" and "You're one of us." Five years after receiving her PhD in history at an elite university in the United States, she failed to get more than one campus interview and still had no job.

In one of her early blog entries she explained the "invisible" feeling she had as an adjunct: "Does it sound too sad/bitter/melodramatic to say that I die a small death every time I feign a brisk cheerfulness as I explain to one of the secretaries in the office that I am So-and-So who needs you to please unlock the door to Office Number XXX so that I can hold the weekly office hours for which I am not paid?"

Yes, it does sound a little melodramatic, until you consider that academics typically spend seven or eight years in graduate school, making next to nothing, so that they can enter a profession that, even if it will not make them wealthy, is supposed to give them a middle-class salary. The website of *The Invisible Adjunct* received about eighteen thousand visitors a month, but its author admitted, "I have to confront the fact that my shelf life has expired, and I'm not going to get a job in the academy."

Compare this situation with the medical profession. Even if medical residents are made to work long hours under difficult conditions, the vast majority of them will get jobs as doctors. The vast majority of, say, PhDs in English literature will not get jobs as full-time English professors. Given that the typical doctoral degree takes so long to complete (during prime job-training and family-forming years), there is a moral problem here. It is no great exaggeration to say, as the Hoover Institution's Peter Berkowitz does, "Many lives are ruined this way."

Marc Bousquet sees a couple of key ironies in the academic job market: getting a PhD now often means the end of an academic career rather than the beginning of one; and the American university, which claims to be an egalitarian institution, relies on people who can afford to take badly paid adjunct teaching positions only because they have another source of income, either from a spouse's job or a second job of their own. Only the independently wealthy can afford to be trained as or even work as an academic.

Moreover, it turns out that women and racial minorities are among the most likely to be hired as adjuncts. The reasons for this are complex, but here are a few. First, women and minorities tend to have graduate degrees from less prestigious institutions. At least initially they usually get jobs at schools lower down on the ladder, where there are fewer tenure-track positions. Second, some women want more flexibility because of family obligations and thus choose to start on the adjunct track; later they find themselves unable to move to the tenure track. Third, some women are pushed into adjunct positions because they gravitate toward "nurturing" roles, concentrating more on teaching and mentoring than on research.

Finally, women tend to gravitate toward fields that hire more adjuncts. As Ashley Finley, a professor of sociology at Dickinson, wrote in a paper called "Women as Contingent Faculty: The Glass Wall" that the proportion of nontenure-track faculty positions was highest in fields like education and fine arts while it was lowest in the natural sciences and engineering. There is no "oversupply" of PhDs in the hard sciences. Those people can always find jobs in the for-profit sector.

Racial minority faculty members are also more likely to be pushed off the tenure track because of the disciplines they pursue. According to Harvard University's Cathy Trower, who has written extensively on tenure, "scholars of color are asked to teach in multiple departments— African American studies and history, for example. Their research can seem out of the mainstream." And thus neither department wants to give them tenure.

The inequities are startling. Women are 10 to 15 percent more likely to occupy contingent faculty positions. They make up more than half of the adjunct faculty and only about a quarter of the tenure-track faculty. Given the gallons of ink spilled in recent years over the difficulties women have advancing in certain parts of the academy, one might think that the issue of contingent faculty at the bottom and the old-boys' tenure club at the top might receive more attention. As Jimeno puts it, "The people I work with write about the marginalization of different social groups. Don't they see it happening right in front of their faces?"

A few senior faculty have become embarrassed by this state of affairs. Peter D. G. Brown, a distinguished service professor of German at SUNY New Paltz, wrote a piece in *Inside Higher Ed* in the spring of 2010 called "Confessions of a Tenured Professor." He says when he began teaching at New Paltz there were only a couple of adjuncts in a department of thirty-five. Now only ten professors remain on the tenure track.

Brown writes, "I must confess that belonging to the de facto elite minority makes me very uneasy. Most tenured faculty view themselves as superior teachers with superior minds. In this view, the arduous six-year tenure process clearly proves that all of us are superior to 'them' and have deservedly earned our superior jobs by our superior gifts and our superior efforts. I must also confess that we tenured faculty really do appreciate the fact that ad-cons have unburdened us from having to teach too many elementary foreign language courses, English composition and the many other tedious introductory, repetitive and highly labor-intensive classes, to which we tenured souls have such a strong aversion that it must be genetic."

Brown is shocked by the working conditions of adjuncts and has served on the founding board of an organization for adjuncts called the New Faculty Majority (which we will shortly discuss at greater length). But Brown is all but alone among tenured faculty who are concerned about adjuncts.

Aside from the hypocrisy of academics who claim concern for society's marginalized while ignoring the lower classes in their midst and what many would deem the unfair treatment of their labor force, is there any compelling reason that universities—as self-interested as any institution—should reconsider their employment policies? Why not staff classes entirely with adjunct labor? Why not give customers essentially the same product at lower cost?

The last question points to a bigger problem, though: Is it the same product? Higher education has gone so far off the rails in recent years that parents and students hardly know what they are supposed to have learned in a freshman composition course or in Sociology 101. And as long as there is a degree waiting at the other end, they hardly care.

But they should. Research shows that in many cases, students faced with adjuncts in the front of their classrooms are getting the short end of the stick. Paul Umbach, a professor of higher education at the University of Iowa, has found that "contingent status, particularly part-time status, is negatively correlated with faculty job performance related to undergraduate education." In a paper for the *Review of Higher Education*, he writes, "Part-time faculty used active and collaborative techniques less frequently than tenure[d] and tenure-track faculty. They also challenged their students significantly less and spent significantly less time preparing for class than their more permanent peers."

Cornell's Ronald Ehrenberg and the University of Minnesota's Liang Zhang, meanwhile, found that the percentage of contingent faculty in an institution had a significant impact on the number of undergraduates who completed their degrees. "Other factors held constant," they write in the *Journal of Human Resources*, "a 10 percentage point increase in the percentage of faculty that is part-time at a public masters' level institution is associated with about a 3 percentage point reduction in the graduation rate of the institution." Even more significantly, "a 10 percentage point increase in the percentage of full-time faculty that are not on tenure-track lines is associated with about a 4.4 percentage point reduction in the graduation rate at the institution."

A 2010 study published in *Education Policy* by Audrey J. Jaeger and M. Kevin Eagan examined six four-year colleges and found that freshmen who have many of their courses taught by adjuncts are less likely to return the following year. At one doctoral institution, for every 10 percent increase in instruction by adjuncts who aren't grad students, the probability that a freshman will come back drops 4 percent. Increasing instruction by graduate students by 10 percent resulted in a 3 percent drop. At a baccalaureate institution the 10 percent increase in adjunct instruction resulted in a 2 percent decline in the likelihood of a freshman returning. In other words, there is a measurable difference in the quality of education received by students who are taught by adjuncts and those taught by full-time tenured or tenure-track faculty.

The research conclusions are not unanimous here. One study by Les Bolt, an associate professor of education at Appalachian State University, found no discernible difference in academic outcomes between students at Blue Ridge Community College who had a great deal of exposure to adjuncts and those who had only a small amount of exposure. Bolt and his coauthor, Hara Charlier (who is interim vice president of instruction at Blue Ridge), found that students who took remedial classes were less likely to complete their degrees, and that adjunct faculty were more likely to teach those classes. The authors speculate that this may be why other scholars have concluded that adjuncts do not teach as well.

In the study by Jaeger and Eagan, the news was not all bad either. The scholars found that at some institutions where adjuncts are better supported professionally, they can have a positive effect on student retention. In other words, when colleges hire people off the tenure track, it is nonetheless possible to treat them decently and professionally. And when that happens, student outcomes are not very different from when students are taught by full-time faculty.

Still, the vast majority of institutions don't treat adjuncts well. The research suggesting a negative effect of adjuncts on education seems to be substantial and to make intuitive sense. When one talks to adjuncts about the hectic pace of their lives—shuttling to multiple institutions, having trouble finding space to hold office hours, and not knowing sometimes until the day before the semester starts whether they will be teaching—the negative effects on students would not be surprising. Adjuncts are generally not as engaged with students as tenure-track faculty members are. This is not because they are less qualified, generally speaking. In fact, as Michigan's Edie Goldenberg points out, since the adjuncts are hired only for their teaching skills and not for research at some institutions, they may well be more effective than their tenured peers. But in most cases, circumstances prevent adjuncts from having more contact with students. And that's a problem that can significantly harm students' prospects for a successful educational experience.

The National Survey of Student Engagement, an annual study of over three hundred thousand students at more than six hundred colleges and universities, has found a higher level of educational engagement for students who interact with faculty outside of the classroom. Alex McCormick, who heads the survey, points out the obvious: "For faculty to interact with students, they have to be there. In the case of some of these adjunct faculty, they may not have an office. Out-of-class engagement becomes thornier if there's not an obvious place a student can go to meet with faculty." Of course, some adjuncts are probably even more committed to engagement with students than senior faculty. McCormick recalls a quip by Clark Kerr, the first chancellor of UC Berkeley: "The nice thing about part-time faculty is that they're around part of the time." Which is to say, the tenured faculty are often missing in action altogether.

But even for someone as interested in teaching as Nancy Jimeno, the situation for students is pretty bleak. Here she is with more than two hundred students in a class, most of whom need personalized attention if they are ever going to learn the kind of reading and writing skills they need to get good jobs. About 20 percent of Cal State Fullerton's full-time freshmen drop out at the end of their first year. Yet neither Jimeno nor her adjunct colleagues have the kind of time to spend with students that might improve those outcomes. The tenured faculty, meanwhile, are busy doing research or teaching advanced classes for the students who have already made it past their introductory courses.

Although it may seem counterintuitive given these statistics about graduation rates, adjuncts also tend to give higher grades than their tenured or tenure-track peers. Since most universities determine whether to rehire a contingent faculty member based on his or her student evaluations, adjuncts must make sure that students like them. Even if a student deserves a lower grade, adjuncts don't want to make waves with the administration or their fellow department members. To avoid student or parent complaints, they often inflate the grade. Mark A. Thoma, an economist at the University of Oregon who has studied this area, has noted two spikes in grade inflation in the past fifty years. One, from the 1960s to the early 1970s, is "usually explained by draft rules for the Vietnam war." That is, you needed a certain GPA to avoid the army, and professors helped students by pushing up their averages.

The second spike begins around 1990, Thoma says. Breaking down grade inflation by instructor at his own university, he found that "it was much higher among assistant professors, adjuncts, TAs, instructors, etc., than for associate or full professors." In other words, tenure made all the difference. Dividing classes into levels 1, 2, and 3, with 3 being the most advanced, he found that full professors gave an A to 26 percent of the 3-level classes while adjuncts gave an A to 38 percent of them. At the lowest level, full professors gave an A to 35 percent of the class while adjuncts gave an A to 42 percent of the class.

Grade inflation, as we know, doesn't do students or parents any favors in the long run. Maybe employers or graduate schools think a student is more qualified, but students may get the impression they've mastered the material when in fact they haven't.

Last year, the American Federation of Teachers (AFT) began a campaign encouraging parents and potential students to "Just Ask" about adjunct faculty. The union suggested posing these four questions:

1) How likely is it that a first- or second-year student at your institution will be taught by full-time, permanent faculty members?
2) What percentage of undergraduate classes and discussion sections are taught by part-time faculty and graduate assistants?
3) How much do part-time faculty make per course at your institution?
4) Are part-time faculty required to hold office hours? Do they get paid to do so, and are they provided suitable office space to meet with students?

The AFT has its own agenda when it comes to ensuring that college faculty are better paid. But in this case the organization is correct that the compensation and treatment of contingent faculty can have a significant effect on a student's college experience.

It seems that a few colleges are growing concerned that parents will ask questions like those listed above. In 2008, the AFT noted that some schools appeared to be lying about the number of adjuncts they employed. The University of Nebraska, Lincoln, for instance, reported to *U.S. News* College Rankings that only 11 of its 1,081 faculty were not full-time. When the AFT blog reported this fishy finding, *Inside Higher Ed* followed up. It turns out that Nebraska was including only tenured or tenure-track faculty who were not full time in its calculations. While *U.S. News* explicitly instructed schools to count adjuncts as well, the rankings editors did not revise the data. Given the fact that most colleges reported that more than 80 percent of their faculty were full-time, it seems likely that other schools were also engaged in some creative accounting.

If you ask people like Marc Bousquet for a solution to the problem of contingent faculty, they will say that nearly everyone should be granted a tenured or tenure-track position. Bousquet compares the role of faculty, at least those at public institutions, to any other public servant. And he believes it's time for taxpayers to be giving adjuncts a better wage: "Unless you are prepared to say that we should pay police officers in the same way, that we should say, 'Okay, 90 percent of police officers should be police students who earn $15,000 for ten years at a time and then 70 percent after that should continue to work for a similar wage with no job security'—unless you're prepared to say that, I can't imagine why you'd think it was just to do this in higher education." Bousquet suggests that the additional money would be worth it, and, if savings had to be found somewhere else, he suggests that money should be taken from schools' lavish building budgets.

Michigan's Edie Goldenberg agrees that there is an argument for ensuring that a higher percentage of university faculty are on the tenure track. But she believes that Bousquet and others who want to give tenure to current adjuncts are wrong. In most cases, she says, they have not earned it. Particularly, she argues, at research institutions, where publication is the key to tenure, adjuncts who have been hired to teach are generally not eligible. So even though a high percentage of adjuncts as teachers seems to have a detrimental effect on student learning, Goldenberg would like to make sure that the adjunct role is reserved for teachers and the tenured role reserved for researchers.

What Goldenberg and Bousquet share is a common belief that the system of tenure is not to blame for the proliferation of adjuncts. (Bousquet believes that tenure is great—we just need to give it to everyone. And Goldenberg thinks tenure is great—but it's only necessary for a specific portion of the faculty population.)

Francis Fukuyama, a professor of political science at the School of Advanced International Studies at Johns Hopkins, disagrees. The institution of tenure and the problems of adjuncts are "absolutely connected," he tells me. "At my school we have a cadre of tenured professors that you can't move out of the way, and a large bulk of teaching done by adjuncts or people who don't have tenure. The disparity in terms of pay and privileges is quite great."

Some professors suggest that if tenure were somehow reformed, then the problems of adjuncts could be solved. Claire Potter, an English professor at Wesleyan who had a very public tenure battle, believes that the trouble for adjuncts stems from the fact that tenured professors are no longer subject to mandatory retirement. She blames "the Reagan Justice

Department" for the problem. In fact, it was the 1986 Age Discrimination Act passed by Congress (which was split between a Republican Senate and a Democratic House) that banned most institutions from allowing any kind of mandatory retirement. Congress allowed an exception for colleges and universities to enforce mandatory retirement of faculty at age seventy until 1994, when they would then be held to the same standard as everyone else.

Leaving aside the political details, it's interesting that a liberal professor like Potter has found a kind of discrimination she likes. But at least she is putting her money where her mouth is. In a recent *New York Times* forum, she announced that she will retire by the spring of 2025, when she will turn sixty-seven: "I believe that if senior scholars offer experience, young PhDs challenge us with new knowledge. Furthermore, while a classroom presence does not necessarily deteriorate with age, we don't always notice, or want to admit it, when we become diminished. Setting a voluntary retirement date, well in advance of any decline, respects this reality."

But why should we have to count on professors themselves to tell us when their performance is beginning to flag? Maybe Claire Potter will still be great at sixty-seven. Why should students be deprived of her teaching simply because some sixty-seven-year-olds aren't good at their jobs anymore? Wouldn't it be more sensible to keep tabs on the performance of faculty in the classroom and then suggest that those who are not up to snuff retire?

Potter's suggestion that tenure used to be fine in the good old days, before it wasn't permanent, is also a little odd. Isn't that the point of tenure? Its permanence? The protection that people claim tenure brings, the guarantees of academic freedom, emanate presumably from the assumption that a tenured position is a permanent one.

As long as academia must abide by federal nondiscrimination laws, tenure will ensure that there is no room for upward mobility in the ivory tower. It is hard to imagine a corporate entity in America that is more stratified than the university.

In a rant on *Inside Higher Ed*, Sabine Hikel, who received her PhD but went to work as a writer and radio producer, encouraged adjuncts to simply get out: "The difficult, crummy truth is out there for everyone to see: You can be the smartest, brightest, most-published person coming out of your degree program and *still* end up without an academic job, simply because the positions aren't there. So why not seize this moment as an opportunity and not an occasion to dig yourself into adjuncting hell? I'm not against optimism. I'm not against holding out for what you really want. But I *am* against the drinking of the academic Kool-Aid."

The low men on the university totem pole may have no chance for advancement. But in many instances they are no less qualified than their tenured colleagues. If a department trusts Nancy Jimeno to teach classes of 250 students on her own, surely she is qualified to be a tenured member of the department. It's true she hasn't published much, but then Cal State Fullerton is considered one of the state's "teaching schools," as opposed to places like Berkeley, which are "research" universities. It's also clear that Jimeno's students need competent teachers who are "available" to the department more than they need people engaged in scholarly publication.

Jimeno, for her part, says she doesn't want tenure: "I think we should be competing with each other, just like a business model." Cathy Trower, who has done significant research at Harvard's School of Education on the attitudes of younger faculty, suggests that this view is not uncommon among them. Speaking of the faculty in Generation X, she says that tenure is not what they're looking for: "They want to be evaluated. They want to work hard, to be productive members of academy." This is, she notes, "a very big shift from older faculty." Trower has done extensive surveys of young faculty, asking, among other things, what is most important to them in a job. "Despite the appeal of the tenure track," she writes in a chapter she contributed to *Questions of Tenure*, "the survey disclosed that faculty and doctoral candidates would select a non-tenure track position under certain conditions related to quality of life: geographic location and the balance between teaching and research."

It's time for younger faculty to realize that Vic Wilcox was right, that holding on to the institution of tenure is not in their best interest. They will continue to be exploited by their employers, receiving low wages for teaching multiple classes at different institutions, and never knowing from one semester to the next whether they can expect another paycheck.

Thanks to tenure's stranglehold on university budgets and the privilege that tenure grants to senior faculty to be "unavailable" for teaching, the population of adjuncts will continue to grow. And as long as this unstable and harried work force takes on a significant percentage of classroom duties, students won't be getting the college education they deserve.

# 5

# The Unions Are Coming

James Turk, the tall, dapper-looking executive director of the Canadian Association of University Teachers, stepped to the podium and began to describe the strength of labor unions on his country's college campuses. The audience of a few hundred American professors and administrators at Hunter College in New York in April 2010 sat rapt as he explained that more than 90 percent of Canadian faculty were unionized, and all but ten of the country's campuses engaged in collective bargaining. Votes on unionization in Canada are "expeditious," in Turk's words, often held within five days of certification. Legislation prevents the universities from hiring "scabs" in case of "work stoppage." Although Canadian schools experienced no strikes in 2009, in 2008 there were five. They typically last two to three weeks, but the longest, a number of years ago, lasted four months. Not only are there no classes during such periods, but the university must also completely shut down. Since the teamsters won't pass picket lines, no deliveries of any sort can be made to campus.

Turk ended his presentation with what was intended, presumably, as a lighthearted story about a strike in eastern Canada, where local mine workers worried that their academic brethren weren't being tough enough on the administration. "We're going to show you how to strike," the mineworkers said. According to Turk, "they put large pipes across the road to block the entrance to the university." Local police then proceeded to shut down the road because of "unsafe conditions."

The audience laughed heartily as Turk's speech, a highlight of the thirty-seventh annual conference of Hunter College's National Center for the Study of Collective Bargaining in Higher Education and the Professions, drew to a close. When he was done, the panel's moderator got up and asked how many members of the audience would like to move to Canada. Almost every hand in the room went up.

American academics aren't emigrating yet, but when it comes to collective bargaining plenty of university campuses are moving northward. Over the past ten years or so, unions have become an increasingly common presence at colleges and universities in the United States. More than 375,000 faculty and graduate students belong to a collective bargaining unit, according to the National Center for the Study of Collective Bargaining in Higher Education and the Professions. That's about a third of the total, and a 24 percent increase in the past decade.

Interestingly, this shift has largely gone unnoticed because it has occurred gradually and in disparate locations. Also, when compared to, say, K–12 teachers or the auto workers, college faculty unions have a relatively small political and economic impact. But their effects are growing. Unionization for college faculty may soon be the order of the day. In a world in which tenure is less common, or if someday it is abolished completely, many professors might turn to the protection of unions for job security.

So now is the time to consider Turk's picture of what union domination of higher education looks like. How would parents and taxpayers take to regular strikes on campus? (Such occurrences are fairly common at European universities too.) Will faculty unions be a force for improving American higher education? Or will organized labor push universities further in the direction of our struggling K–12 education system? Is mass unionization better or worse than tenure as a means for giving job security to college faculty?

Before we get back to the United States, it might be useful to hear from one of James Turk's Canadian colleagues. Lorne Carmichael, an economist at Queens University in Ontario, says that the unionization of his campus has "opened his eyes" to the problems created by organizing faculty. "In a unionized environment, it's the political people, the people who want to sit on boards and committees," who have the most influence—not the people who do the teaching or research. And Carmichael believes that the unions are protecting the least competent faculty members: "You would get more output from professors if you didn't have unionization."

Unionization on American college campuses began in the early 1900s with the founding of the American Federation of Teachers Local 33 at Howard University, according to Timothy Reese Cain, a professor of educational organization and leadership at the University of Illinois. But by the 1920s membership plummeted, a result of the popular (and not altogether unfounded) sentiment that universities were leaning toward socialism. (Such concerns don't seem to have much effect on faculty today.) The movement experienced a brief surge again in the 1930s, but unions still didn't have the right to collective bargaining on most campuses. In the 1960s, with the rise of community colleges, the AFT finally gained a large national foothold. Meanwhile, the National Education Association (NEA) grew popular on some four-year campuses, particularly at teachers colleges.

In contrast to the NEA and the AFT, the American Association of University Professors opposed collective bargaining for the first several decades of its existence on the commonly held belief that universities were not corporations and faculty were not employees in the same sense as factory workers.[1] The AAUP also wanted to distinguish its members from teachers at the elementary and secondary levels. In 1919, the AAUP president, Arthur Lovejoy, told his colleagues that it would be

---

1. From its founding, the AAUP was a professional organization like the American Bar Association—not a union. But then it began to offer its services as a collective bargaining agent to some campuses.

better if faculty were "organized in an independent professional body rather than as part of a national federation of labor unions." And when at its annual meeting in 1972 the association's members finally voted to change its stance to favor unionization, controversy erupted. The following year, the group lost ten thousand members.

The first half of the 1970s was a time of great uncertainty for the professoriate, particularly at public universities where budget cuts were the order of the day. The period saw a substantial upsurge in faculty unionization—schools from the University of Massachusetts to the California State University system organized at that time. Those unions remain some of the most powerful in higher education today. The unionization process often began with some issue of discontent on the part of the faculty. Then a faculty senate or similar body would vote on whether it supported unionization. Assuming that it was legal, different unions—the AAUP, the AFT, the NEA, or a state employees union—would then compete to become the bargaining agent for that school. They would try to get faculty to sign enough cards to certify a union election on campus.

The experience of faculty at the University of Rhode Island was not atypical. As Gordon Arnold documents in his book *The Politics of Faculty Unionization*, Rhode Island faculty were upset over their salaries in 1970 and were further provoked by an incident in which the president decided to cancel a controversial class (though he quickly reinstated it). As of 1966, the faculty in Rhode Island had been permitted under state law to enter into collective bargaining. The faculty senate at URI voted in favor of unionizing and then put it to a vote of the entire faculty. Of the 600 professors, 180 signed cards endorsing a collective bargaining election. Some opposition to unionization was voiced from a group called Faculty for Professional Freedom, as well as from a group at Rhode Island's business school, which assumed, not incorrectly, that unionization would have a leveling effect on the various disciplines and would actually mean a lowering of their salaries. Ultimately, two unions seriously competed to be the bargaining agent—the AAUP and the University of Rhode Island

Professional Association. In the end, the latter threw its support behind the AAUP and the faculty voted to unionize, 293 to 289.

Still, unionization was anathema to faculty at most higher-level four-year institutions. As Arnold writes, it was the "prevailing view that American higher education was a meritocracy, and that union impulses were the result, at least in part, of professors who could not compete with their elite peers." In a study for the Carnegie Commission on Higher Education, Seymour Martin Lipset and Everett C. Ladd Jr. concluded that faculty of "low scholarly achievement give greater backing to the principles of collective bargaining."

The oddity of forming unions for what were supposed to be high-ranking professionals was not lost even on the lay observer. As a 1976 story in the *New York Times* put it, faculty were "accustomed to looking with disdain at those who earn their living with muscles rather than their minds." And unions were for the muscular.

Indeed, as rapidly as unions spread during the 1970s, Arnold maintains that support for them among the general population was not "very strong or deep." While many observers of higher education during that decade envisioned, according to Arnold, "a world in which faculty unions would continue to spread across the pantheon of American colleges and universities," things did not turn out that way. "A decade later the movement would significantly slow down." A shift in public opinion away from labor—the air traffic controllers' strike in 1981 was one low point—as well as an important court decision (which we will discuss momentarily) did not bode well for unions on college campuses.

But, like so many ideas from the 1970s, campus unionization has today come roaring back. More and more faculty have begun to share Cain's attitude that "faculty have, for the most part, been employees, we just don't like to admit it."

Several factors have made college campuses ripe targets for organized labor lately. First and foremost, conditions for adjuncts and contingent labor, as already noted, have worsened significantly. Low salaries, long hours, a lack of benefits, and no job security make even the most reluctant professors into union activists.

Take Matt Williams. An adjunct faculty member at the University of Akron until recently, Williams came to some prominence when he resigned over objections to a new university policy requiring all employees to submit DNA samples. (The university claimed it had not actually collected the samples, and it would do so only to conduct criminal background checks. Nevertheless, the requirement is illegal under the recently passed Genetic Information Nondiscrimination Act.) The university initially rehired Williams to teach the following semester, but then it rescinded that contract on grounds that his prior resignation made him unreliable. Because he is a nontenure-track faculty member and has no union to support him, Williams has little recourse.

Williams's case has now been taken up by the American Civil Liberties Union. He maintains that he was concerned about the volatile condition of adjunct faculty at his school even before the DNA-sample controversy began. When he went to purchase health insurance from the University of Akron a couple of years ago, he found that it wasn't a viable option. According to Williams, an adjunct who was teaching three credits less than a full-time load would have had to pay 20 percent more than his gross salary to purchase the least expensive health-care plan.

Williams's nonadjunct colleagues don't have to worry about such costs. Not only do they have job security and decent salaries and benefits, but under state law the senior faculty are represented by a union. In an effort to correct this disparity, Williams is pushing a bill in the Ohio legislature to ensure that adjunct faculty are also represented.

Even so, Williams insists that he is an unlikely union activist. A member of the executive committee of his local Republican Party, Williams says he has mixed feelings on the issue of organizing. "I'm conflicted as a matter of principle," he notes. "I'm not a real big fan of unionization."

He proceeds to tell me a story about a nearby mayor who was censured after he fixed a manhole cover that he found askew. "Under the union contract, four or five people were required to be there," sighs Williams. He is familiar with (and believes) a lot of "those stories about people being paid to sit around and play cards." "It gives me pause to take a step in that direction," but, he wonders, "What are the alternatives?"

Williams says that—like most fiscal conservatives—he has no problem with executive-level compensation, but when the university president makes a thousand times what part-time employees do, he thinks "it's a matter of people lining their own pockets." It is true that despite budget cuts across the state in the last couple of years, the salaries of the presidents of Ohio's public colleges have continued to grow, and the schools have continued to add more administrators to the payroll. Whatever his objections to unionization in theory, he believes that corporations and universities often "get the union they deserve."

It's not only that faculty, particularly those at the bottom of the ladder, feel they need labor unions to defend them. It's also that "big labor" has begun to look for more targets in white-collar professions. As the United States has become an information economy and factory jobs have disappeared, so the membership of labor unions has declined. Only 12.4 percent of the country's workforce, or 16.1 million workers, belonged to a labor union in 2008, down from a peak of 28.3 percent in 1954.

In 2008, the American Federation of Teachers announced a joint campaign with the American Association of University Professors to unionize more public universities. "We don't have a number in mind," Sandra Schroeder, chairman of the AFT's higher education council, said, but it's "as many as we possibly can."

Public university professors not only fit with the new union profile of white-collar workers, but the fact that they are state employees is also in line with the current union model. According to a 2010 report from the Bureau of Labor Statistics, the majority of the country's union members are government workers, rather than private-sector workers, for the first time in history. Then there is also the fact that most college faculty are sympathetic to union politics. The anti-corporate tone on many campuses and the left-leaning political views of college professors make them open to the union message.

College faculty may be perfect targets for the unions, but unless they personally have something to gain, it's not clear they will buy in. Matt Williams's experience seems to bear this out. At the University of Akron, Williams says, he has received little support from the school's senior faculty for his efforts to organize the adjuncts. "I've not found that the full-time faculty, as measured by their willingness to get involved, has been terribly concerned. They're unwilling to get their hands dirty."

As mentioned earlier, one exception has been Peter Brown of SUNY New Paltz, who has registered his irritation with tenured faculty on this matter. He was even more annoyed to find that the union for university faculty in New York, United University Professions, had yet to establish a minimum salary for adjuncts. Which is not all that surprising given what else he learned: "Our UUP chapter's 'Part-Time Concerns Rep' was actually a tenured professor who was out of the country for a year doing research." For most senior academics, securing benefits for adjuncts is not high on the priority list.

It has been thirty years since the Supreme Court all but banned the unionization of faculty on private campuses in a case we will discuss shortly. At public universities, the biggest obstacle to more widespread unionization of higher education, though, is the patchwork of different labor regulations that govern college campuses in different states. In fact, the authorities that make those rules also vary considerably. Labor boards, state legislatures, and governors have varying degrees of power to determine where unions can take root. Some states allow part-time faculty unions; some, like Ohio, do not. Wisconsin has allowed some of its campuses to organize for decades, but it was only in 2009 that the governor signed an order as part of his budget allowing for the University of Wisconsin at Madison faculty to do so. Some unions are associated with the American Federation of Teachers. Some are chapters of the American Association of University Professors. Some are completely independent. Some schools have separate bargaining units for full-time and part-time faculty while at other schools they are all in the same group.

If labor cannot make these rules uniform across state borders— a tough order, particularly in the so-called right-to-work states—they are now at least trying to pursue a clear set of goals on behalf of faculty, wherever they live. The FACE (Faculty and College Excellence) initiative, a joint effort of the AFT and the AAUP, is pursuing two major objectives: "Achieving full equity in compensation for contingent faculty members; and ensuring that 75 percent of undergraduate classes are taught by full-time tenure[d] and tenure-track faculty and that qualified contingent faculty have the opportunity to move into such positions as they become available."

At the biennial meeting of the Coalition of Contingent Academic Labor in August 2010, Cary Nelson, head of the AAUP, told his audience, "The only goal worth fighting for is full justice for all who teach." He explained that "the first fundamental step is to give people lifetime job security and then build from that." He wants to make all those who serve in contingent roles eligible for tenure, even those adjuncts whose primary function is teaching, not research.

A representative of the New Faculty Majority, a coalition of adjunct faculty, has offered a similar plan for the next twenty years whereby adjuncts would be offered equal pay, benefits, and the right to tenure. But it proposes to disconnect tenure from higher salaries, thereby encouraging administrators to hire more people on the tenure track without significantly increasing costs immediately. Both NFM and AAUP continue to pursue tenure as the holy grail for their members.

At the 2009 conference on collective bargaining at Hunter College, Randi Weingarten, head of the American Federation of Teachers, told the audience that "there is a real dilemma in higher education when almost three-quarters of the academy is made of contingent faculty and almost half of undergraduate courses are taught by adjuncts." She emphasized that she didn't want to suggest "adjuncts are bad," but she argued that higher education is at a "tipping point." With so many adjunct faculty, she wondered (a bit melodramatically), "What does it mean in terms of kids having some adults they can rely on, not just someone who is in and out?"

But unlike the AAUP and the New Faculty Majority, the AFT seems to be going down two roads at the same time, on the one hand pushing universities to add more tenure-track positions but on the other hand acknowledging that there are a lot of insecure adjuncts on campus now who feel they need representation. In 2007, Scott Jaschik of *Inside Higher Ed* reported on the AFT's conference of higher-education union leaders in Portland, Oregon. According to Jascik, the AFT acknowledged at the meeting "that relying on the tenure system to protect professors' academic freedom doesn't work when more and more faculty members don't have, and may never have, tenure." Union leaders "were briefed on contracts for adjuncts that have won nontenure-track faculty members 'continuous employment status' (not identical to tenure, but much closer to tenure than the typical semester-to-semester employment status of a typical adjunct)."

The AFT policy statement released at the meeting outlined the ways that nontenure-track faculty could be guaranteed academic freedom. And here, it seems, the AFT shows its true colors as a union whose origins do not lie in higher education. The AFT is basically offering its members academic freedom by means other than tenure, severing a connection that is sacrosanct in higher education.

On some level it's not surprising that the AFT would compromise this fundamental principle of college faculty in the service of growing its numbers. The unions see a real opportunity on public campuses. They can use the lobbying power they have already built in state capitals and Washington to push for greater freedom to organize. And they know that if they can get legislators to allow for more organization on campus, many of the lower-tier schools will be happy to join. Finally, if the fastest-growing segment of faculty are adjuncts, the unions know they have a bright future on campus.

If public universities are fertile ground for union recruitment, private campuses have been all but shut down as a source. In 1980, the Supreme Court decided the case of *NLRB v. Yeshiva University*, ruling that, contrary to the view of the National Labor Relations Board, the faculty of Yeshiva did not have the right to organize. The court reasoned that under the National Labor Relations Act, the faculty were like "managers" and thus not entitled to the protections of a union. (The NLRA governs only the private sector, not the public.)

As Justice Powell wrote in his majority opinion, "The controlling consideration in this case is that the faculty of Yeshiva University exercise authority which in any other context unquestionably would be managerial. Their authority in academic matters is absolute. They decide what courses will be offered, when they will be scheduled, and to whom they will be taught. They debate and determine teaching methods, grading policies, and matriculation standards. They effectively decide which students will be admitted, retained, and graduated. On occasion their views have determined the size of the student body, the tuition to be charged, and the location of a school. When one considers the function of a university, it is difficult to imagine decisions more managerial than these. To the extent the industrial analogy applies, the faculty determines within each school the product to be produced, the terms upon which it will be offered, and the customers who will be served."

In addition to the "managerial" duties carried out by the faculty, the Court also suggested that the institution of tenure can serve to "insulate the professor from some of the sanctions applied to an industrial manager who fails to adhere to company policy." In other words, tenure is yet another reason that faculty may not unionize.

In the thirty years since the *Yeshiva* decision, the makeup of university faculty has changed significantly. And the duties and benefits that accrue to professors have also changed. Adjunct professors would rightly contend that they don't in any way resemble management, and that Justice Powell's description of the job of a professor is not one they recognize. Thus they should be allowed to unionize.

In 2002, professors at LeMoyne-Owen College, a private school in Tennessee, voted 43 to 4 to make their faculty senate their collective bargaining agent. The NLRB's regional acting director in Memphis at first ruled against this move, citing the *Yeshiva* decision. But a few months later, the board itself found that the LeMoyne professors "neither possess absolute control over any facet of the school's operations nor effectively recommend policies affecting its administration." Nonetheless the District of Columbia Court of Appeals was unconvinced and remanded the decision to the NLRB for further explanation. This attempt to apply Powell's logic to allow for the unionization of faculty so far seems to have gone nowhere.

In another speech at the 2010 Hunter College collective bargaining conference, Wilma Liebman, the NLRB chair and one of only two members of the board for the past three years, expressed her frustration with the courts on this point. The board is "facing some skepticism, if not hostility, by the courts about collective bargaining in this area," she complained.

Speaking only days after President Obama had made two recess appointments to the board, including Craig Becker, former general counsel for the Service Employees International Union, Liebman suggested that the board would take a more "dynamic" approach to such cases. She worried that "confidence in the NLRB and federal labor law have diminished in last few decades." She said it's "become more obvious to many people that the [NLRA] statute isn't working the way it was supposed to. We need to look at the importance of the statute and make it more vibrant."

Whether one wants Liebman's efforts to succeed or not, it does seem that the *Yeshiva* decision left lower-ranking college faculty with some ground to stand on. As Justice Powell wrote, "There thus may be institutions of higher learning, unlike Yeshiva, where the faculty are entirely or predominantly nonmanagerial. There also may be faculty members at Yeshiva and like universities who properly could be included in a bargaining unit. It may be that a rational line could be drawn between tenured and untenured faculty members, depending upon how a faculty is structured and operates. But we express no opinion on these questions."

Despite what seems to be an open legal question, contingent faculty have made little headway on private campuses. Graduate students, on the other hand, are a different story. Graduate students who teach courses do not fall under the provisions of the *Yeshiva* decision. The question of whether they may collectively bargain rests on whether the court primarily sees their relationship to the university as educational or economic. (Making this determination is the NLRB's task, but it must fall within the bounds of Supreme Court precedent.)

In 1991, graduate students at Yale went on strike to form a union. The school's custodial, clerical, and food-service staff joined them. With 45 percent of the school's unionized staff staying off the job, many university functions ground to a halt. The strike ultimately resulted in a small pay raise for graduate students and the establishment of a teacher-training program. In 1995, Yale graduate students struck again, this time because the administration wouldn't recognize an election that endorsed the Graduate Employees and Students Organization (GESO) as the students' bargaining unit. Again they made some small gains, including a tuition waiver for all beginning PhD students. But their quest for recognition of the union by the university went nowhere. All along, the administration claimed that the students were primarily students, not employees, and thus had no right to unionize under the provisions of the National Labor Relations Act.

But in 2001 the situation for graduate students at Yale and other private universities began to turn around. That's when the NLRB (at the time ruled by a President Clinton–appointed majority) ruled that students at New York University *did* have the right to unionize. "We reject the contention of the Employer and several of the amici that, because the graduate assistants may be 'predominantly students,' they cannot be statutory employees," the decision read. And so NYU became the first private university in the country to approve a union contract.

It turned out to be a fairly small step forward, though, as in 2004, the NLRB effectively changed its mind with a ruling against graduate students at Brown University who wanted to form a union of their own. And the NYU administration declined to renew their contract with the union, knowing they were now on firm legal ground. Liebman dissented on the Brown decision, writing that the majority "errs in seeing the academic world as somehow removed from the economic realm that labor law addresses—as if there was no room in the ivory tower for a sweatshop."

Graduate students at Columbia, NYU, and Yale, among other schools, have continued to press their administrations to engage in collective bargaining ever since, without much success. But now there is a new game in town. Because the NLRB is typically made up of five political appointees, with a majority given to members whose party is in the White House, the decisions can change every few years without rhyme or reason.

Not only are the new NLRB appointments likely to be more sympathetic to the graduate students, but President Obama himself has also supported graduate student unionization. In 2008, he introduced a bill, along with then-senators Hillary Clinton and Edward Kennedy, that would eliminate any ambiguity in the NLRA. The language read, "[T]he term 'employee' includes a student enrolled at [a private] institution of higher education . . . who is performing work for remuneration at the direction of the institution, whether or not the work relates to the student's course of study."

Liberal politicians may think this a good cause, but there is not a great deal of support on campus for graduate student unions. Many of the graduate students themselves have chosen not to become involved. And the *Yale Daily News* even editorialized against it. "Graduate students come to Yale as students, not as workers, and while here, their services as workers, no matter how valuable, are still secondary to their role as students," the editorial declared. It also suggested that the strikes were doing little more than disrupting education—after six strikes in fifteen years, the administration hardly seems any more likely to recognize the union.

Public opinion is not much with the graduate students either. As often as not, parents assume that graduate students are lazy twenty-somethings who just want to stay in school, sheltered from the real world for as long as possible. They would laugh, perhaps rightly, at Liebman's suggestion that universities can house teaching "sweatshops" on campus. And maybe there is something to their suspicions. But to say that the relationship between graduate students and the administration is not primarily an economic one would be a stretch in most cases.

In fact, graduate students are the engine that allows most large universities to run the way they do. Since senior tenured professors often have little or no interest in teaching large introductory courses like freshman composition, those duties fall on the graduate students.

In theory, of course, these graduate students are not simply thrown into the classroom to do their labors. They are supposed to be apprentices, learning how to teach. John Silber, who was president of Boston University when its graduate students tried to form a union in the late 1970s, thinks it is the role of the department chair and the administration to make sure that graduate students are students. "When I was in charge, particularly as a department chairman [at the University of Texas]," he tells me, "I would never assign teaching assistants to a faculty member unless that faculty member taught a seminar in directed teaching or a seminar in the introduction to teaching. And I would insist that they meet with their teaching assistants for a seminar every single week. They would discuss how the course was going, get the students involved in writing the examinations and show them how to write examinations, and also show them how to grade papers and how to evaluate these assignments. All of that is an important part of instruction." In other words, being a teaching assistant is only a part of your "education" as a graduate student if the school is actually teaching you how to be a teaching assistant.

On the other hand, Silber has little sympathy for universities whose graduate students act as employees: "If you give them a free hand and put them in a course just as if they were an instructor, with no guidance or anything else, well, then you run into a problem."

Indeed, the problem of graduate student unionization goes back to the question of to what extent universities value teaching. A graduate student, as Silber points out, is supposed to be learning not only more advanced subject matter in his or her discipline. He is supposed to be learning how to teach. To the extent that the university uses graduate students merely as low-cost labor—throwing any warm body into a classroom of freshmen—then, as Matt Williams says, they get the union they deserve.

Since many public university systems have been organized for more than thirty years now, it's worth examining what kinds of effects unions have had on the faculty. Here are a few examples.

California began allowing unionization for its public university campuses in the early 1970s, but there were different conditions offered for the California state system than for the University of California system. At the former, if a majority of the campuses voted to unionize, they would all be unionized. At the latter, each campus took a vote on its own. As a result, for the past quarter-century Cal State has had collective bargaining and UC has not.

Charles Baird, an emeritus economics professor at Cal State East Bay, was on campus for several years before the vote to unionize took place, and lived and taught under the rules of the California Faculty Association for a number of decades afterward. Baird describes a situation in which the administration of the school was so fearful of starting a fight with the Cal State union that they allowed the whole business school to go to pot. By the early 2000s the school was in danger of losing its accreditation, according to Baird, who became its associate dean in 2005.

A new dean was brought in to ready the school for its accreditation review by the Association to Advance Collegiate Schools of Business. He offered reduced teaching loads to faculty who published their work in reputable research journals, he arranged for summer research grants and bonuses to faculty who submitted good proposals, and he tried to put some teeth into the five-year post-tenure reviews that had become basically pro forma. But, Baird writes, "The CFA blocked the incentives on the grounds that they created invidious distinctions between faculty members." He notes, "Such rewards for excellence undermine the solidarity that unions always seek."

As for the post-tenure review, the union blocked that on the grounds that it did not take account of teaching, only publication. Leave aside for a moment the fact that the AACSB places a high value on publication when it comes to accreditation, so if a school wants to be accredited by them it has to do the same. It doesn't take much digging to see how disingenuous the union was being. The union also worked to do away with the university's outstanding teaching award because of the merit payment that came attached to it.

In the end, the business school at California East Bay was placed on probation for one year. Rather than trying to influence the faculty they had, the administrators instead hired a whole group of new PhDs who were "up" on the latest research and automatically considered academically qualified by the accreditor. The school had to find a way, albeit an expensive one, to work around the union.

The story of CSU is fairly typical of what happens when a campus is unionized. Bruce Cameron, a professor at Regent University School of Law and a staff attorney at the National Right to Work Legal Defense Fund, has been representing professors caught on the wrong side of unions for decades now. In the 1970s he represented a faculty member at the University of Massachusetts who was supposed to receive a merit bonus for having a paper published in a reputable journal. The union eliminated his bonus (and all merit-based bonuses) and forced him to pay union dues as well. Says Cameron, "Unionization doesn't do anything for senior faculty. It only creates peril for their job if they don't pay money to the union."

In Cameron's experience, the faculty and graduate students in math and the hard sciences often object most to this "collectivization" because "they are working with grants and they can have fairly good salaries." According to the unions, a university would expect to get a faculty member in the hard sciences for the same price as one in the humanities. But, of course, this shows a complete lack of understanding of the market, in which there is a glut of humanities professors while the hard sciences faculty members have plenty of other well-paying options open to them outside academia. According to *Inside Higher Ed*, the graduate student union at New York University, for instance, did not include most science students, and the math students ended their participation in the strike long before the rest of the students did.

Recently, Cameron was representing a couple of graduate students in the UMass faculty union, which is affiliated with the United Auto Workers. The union was charging the students dues for *all* the UAW collective bargaining costs within that unit. But the unit also included rug weavers and child-care providers. The students wondered why they should be charged for the costs associated with these other workers when their interests seem to have little relation to them. As Cameron notes, "The unions like to say they're making your life better, but that's rarely the case."

The compression of wages caused by campus unionization occurs not only because of the elimination of merit awards for pay. And not only because unions try to eliminate pay distinctions among faculty in different disciplines. The unions also try to equalize compensation across campuses. In the winter of 2010, the state of New York began an epic battle over how to close its $2 billion budget gap. One proposal floated by Lieutenant Governor Richard Ravitch and some members of the legislature was to charge different tuition rates to students who attend New York's schools. Under the proposal, the various SUNY campuses would each decide on their own tuition rates rather than having a uniform one.

The United University Professions, the collective bargaining unit that represents all the faculty at SUNY schools, opposed the legislation, which was referred to as the Public Higher Education Empowerment Act. At a rally in Albany, the president of the union, Philip Smith, told the crowd that "this should really be called the Public Higher Education Endangerment and Injury Act." He warned that the resulting tuition hikes not only could put "SUNY out of reach for many students, it would also allow the state to shirk its responsibility for funding its public university. . . . And giving campuses the power to negotiate their own leases, contracts, and joint ventures opens the door to revenue-making deals that puts students a distant second."

In the spring the faculty at Stony Brook University, which with the University of Buffalo are the two SUNY schools designated as research universities by the American Association of Universities, met with UUP representatives to object to the union's position on differential tuition. Stony Brook's $6,000 tuition is about $5,000 lower than that of flagship universities in nearby states, and the faculty there think it's time they charge students what a Stony Brook education is worth, not what a Fredonia State education is worth.

In a letter to Smith, Michael A. Frohman, chairman of the Department of Pharmacological Sciences, wrote in support of differential tuition: "We must find other sources of support, or enter a period of decline to mediocrity not worthy of or capable of meeting the needs of our state and residents."

It is not the case, of course, that the UUP leadership cares about student pocketbooks whereas the Stony Brook faculty are just a bunch of heartless scrooges. Union leaders would be happy to get more money for faculty, but they want it to come from Albany, not from individual students. As Cameron notes, "The union is always worried about leaving these questions to the vagaries of the market." It doesn't want to see distinctions made among better and worse campuses and, thereby, among the better and worse faculties. Those distinctions would undermine union solidarity.

As John Simpson, president of the University of Buffalo, tells me, "unionization runs contrary to what you're socialized to do if you're a researcher. The notion of belonging to a herd seems on the face of it inappropriate."

K. C. Johnson, a professor at the City University of New York, finds "the principle of unionization to be anti-meritocratic. The unions want wages assigned on the basis of seniority." A professor who has won a Pulitzer Prize and one who has never published a book will be paid the same amount if they have been at the university for the same amount of time. Johnson wonders in such a situation, "Who is the union supposed to represent?"

Simpson echoes Johnson's complaint that, thanks to union rules, the faculty at his university cannot be rewarded much for merit. They have each gotten 4 percent raises over the past few years, but only one-quarter of that is based on actual accomplishment. In the end, the New York legislature did not include any of the reform provisions in the final budget it passed in August 2010. Given the unions' power in Albany, they're unlikely to be enacted in the future.

It would be hard to imagine someone like Michael Frohman or many of his Stony Brook colleagues at Hunter's collective bargaining conference. The academics in attendance are not generally members of elite institutions. They are certainly not the media's image of college professors. Academic unions, as significant a force as they have become, are largely the product of lower-tier campuses.

If you spend an hour at the conference, you might suspect that a line between college faculty and blue-collar workers has become blurred, that in the long run the camaraderie described by James Turk between the miners and the faculty in Canada will not be the exception. Take someone like Dee Montgomery Smith, president of Chemeketa Part-Time Education Association at Chemeketa Community College in Oregon. During a panel at the 2009 conference, she aggressively warned the audience that she might "sound nasty" after "fifteen months of negotiation" with her school's administration. But she was convinced that her colleagues were being led "like sheep to slaughter."

Maria Maisto, president of the New Faculty Majority, tells me that when it comes to considering which school is the model for how faculty should be treated, she says "the one institution we always point to is Vancouver Community College in British Columbia." Maisto, an adjunct faculty member at the University of Akron, can say this with a straight face, but it's hard to imagine someone at the University of Michigan, Ann Arbor, suggesting the same thing. Vancouver Community College will be the model only for some kinds of faculty.

Maisto's group, the New Faculty Majority, is not a union. It is a loosely affiliated national group for adjuncts and contingent faculty who are looking for a better deal from their universities. NFM's popularity is a sign both that a great many campuses are ripe for unionization and that unionization is not the answer for all the faculty complaints. Many of their members are also members of unions—though some are in "mixed units," meaning that the leaders are supposed to represent the interests of contingent faculty and full-time faculty at the same time. That's not always possible, as Peter Brown found when he looked into the question of who was representing part-timers.

Even James Turk suggests that unions are not the solution for everything, and he complains that Canada's contingent faculty continue to be "exploited" despite their union membership. There are few strictly egalitarian systems of governance out there. So there's always going to be some group on the bottom.

K. C. Johnson has not been particularly impressed with the protections of a union. When, as an untenured professor, he refused to participate in a politically motivated post-9/11 "teach-in" at Brooklyn College, he became a sort of pariah in his department. Johnson was denied tenure shortly thereafter, and the union that officially represented him refused to come to his defense. He had to hire his own attorney to press his case.

When it comes to job security, it seems, faculty members and education experts differ on how the protections of a union compare to the protections of tenure. Wesleyan's Claire Potter says, "For my money, I would give up tenure in a second if I could join a good union." She believes that "collective bargaining is good for the workplace because you have to have cause to fire someone." Since most administrators would say that trying to fire someone with tenure (with or without cause) is a pretty tough order, it's not clear what Potter would gain from an alternative situation.

Chester Finn, former assistant secretary of education, for his part is not sure which is worse—tenure or mass unionization—in terms of undermining the quality of higher education. But he rightly notes that to have both in operation at some universities "is absolutely outrageous." If he had to make a distinction between what tenure accomplishes and what unionization does, he says, "tenure is supposed to protect the individual. And unionization is supposed to create group equality." In this understanding, though, Johnson presumably would have been protected. If he was part of the group—no matter his competence or his politics—the union should have been at his side. But as Johnson and others have noted, union leadership are often among the most radical people on campus, even on radical campuses.

Some observers worry that unions create more problems outside the realm of job protection than tenure does. Peter Kirsanow, a former member of the National Labor Relations Board, says that while both tenure and unionization make it very hard to get rid of bad faculty members, he thinks that those engaged in collective bargaining will inevitably try to influence parts of the university that lie outside wages and job security. The unions "will want to get into curricula, class schedules, grading norms, etc.," which could have an even more detrimental effect on university life than tenure.

And Johnson agrees. In an article on the "perils of academic unions," he wrote, "Since few academics enter the profession to become labor activists, those who gravitate toward union service are more likely to fall on the fringes of a professoriate that is ideologically one-sided." As part of its campaign to move classes off campus a few years ago, the NYU student union paid to hold classes in American Communist party headquarters.

Will the increasing presence of unions on campus result in a more highly politicized environment than the tenure system has already created? Will unions push the professoriate into further mediocrity? Will they deepen the divide between the humanities and the hard sciences? The answer to all these questions is probably.

Will things be worse if the tenure system is somehow replaced with mass unionization? It's certainly possible.

What is certain, though, is that more and more faculty members are fleeing into the arms of unions as the tenure system weakens. It's hard to blame adjuncts or even graduate students for thinking they need union protection, given their current work conditions. And given the goals of big labor, it's easy to understand that these additional members will be warmly welcomed. All of which is good reason to come up with a sensible alternative to both systems, one that offers reasonable salaries to talented people without the guarantee (through tenure or unions) of a job for life.

# 6

# University Politics and the Politics of the University

It probably didn't surprise anyone who follows the politics of higher education that during the 2008 presidential campaign college professors donated more money to President Obama than they did to John McCain. But it might come as a shock that they donated *eight times as much* to the president. College professors have long tilted leftward, but the campaign-donation gap has actually grown significantly over the past several elections, according to the *Chronicle of Higher Education*. In 2000, professors actually gave slightly more to George W. Bush than to Al Gore. The year 2004 was really the tipping point, apparently, when professors gave four times as much to John Kerry as they did to President Bush.

In interviews shortly after the election, some of the donors explained their reasoning. "I gave out of a sense of urgency," John A. McCumber, a professor of Germanic languages at UCLA, told the *Chronicle*. "The country can't go on this way." He charged that Republicans "have opted for an anti-mind strategy." Carl Shapiro, a professor of business at UC Berkeley, told the same reporter that Republicans' approach to science is "offensive . . . for those of us whose lives are about inquiry and study and evidence and thought."

In article after article and survey after survey, the professoriate reveals a universally negative opinion about Republicans, conservatives, evangelical Christians, and the right in general. When it comes to politics, as Hank Brown, the former president of the University of Colorado has put it, "There is greater unanimity of opinion on college campuses than in any other portion of society." The tenure process has contributed to this unanimity and even cemented it in place.

Just how politically radical is the university? Take Henry A. Giroux, whose book *The University in Chains: Confronting the Military-Industrial-Academic Complex* is something of a clarion call for campus leftists. When his manifesto was published in 2007, he told *Inside Higher Ed* that he worried about "the transformation of higher education into a 'militarized knowledge factory.'" He cites not only the presence of ROTC on some campuses but the proliferation of Pentagon-funded research projects. "Faculty are lured," he says, "to the Department of Defense, the Pentagon, and various intelligence agencies either to procure government jobs or to apply for grants to support individual research in the service of the national security state and the U.S. government's commitment to global military supremacy."

But it is not only the U.S. government that's controlling American universities, according to Giroux: "Corporations, the national security state, the Pentagon, powerful Christian evangelical groups, nongovernment agencies, and enormously wealthy right-wing individuals and institutions have created powerful alliances—the perfect storm so to speak—that are truly threatening the freedoms and semi-autonomy of American universities."

Giroux is certainly on the fringe of academic debate. In fact, there are plenty of respected "mainstream" academics who would argue that the complaint about the university tilting left is inaccurate—evidence from the voting booth notwithstanding.

In his recent book, *No University Is an Island*, Cary Nelson, president of the American Association of University Professors, goes to great lengths to show that college campuses are often inhospitable to people of *all* political stripes. *Everyone* can be a victim. He criticizes figures on the right like former 1960s radical David Horowitz and Anne Neal of the American Council of Trustees and Alumni for their "determination to exaggerate or misrepresent their own and other people's psychological alienation." Nelson explains that "people on the Left are just as likely to be besieged."

He cites, for instance, the experience of blogger Michael Berubé, a professor of American studies at Penn State. Berubé argued that in the wake of 9/11, military action in Afghanistan was necessary to remove the Taliban. Despite the fact that, as Nelson notes, Berubé "did not endorse the Bush administration's wantonly brutal, failed tactics there," he found himself a "pariah" among many on the campus left.

Nelson also apparently had a hard time after endorsing military action in Afghanistan, while opposing the war in Iraq. He recalls that "there was no social space in which to give qualified support to one military action and thoroughly condemn the other without being treated with contempt." (A lack of social space is code, presumably, for not being invited to the right dinner parties.)

That Nelson has chosen these examples is revealing. After all, they do not show that the left is not the dominant force on campus. They show that the left is *so* dominant that it does not abide the slightest departure from its pacifist orthodoxy. If even Cary Nelson and Michael Berubé are not pure enough for the campus left, what does that say about campus politics?

As blogger Erin O'Connor explains, the way you view campus politics all depends on where you draw the boundaries of reasonable political discourse. In their book *Closed Minds*, the political scientists Bruce Smith, Jeremy Mayer, and A. Lee Fritschler ask professors how they would define themselves politically. About 19 percent define themselves as "strongly liberal," 42 percent as moderately liberal, and 19 percent as "middle of the road." The authors conclude that the ratio of Democrats to Republicans is four to one—not really much of a change over the past few decades, they say. But middle of the road is a pretty vague category.

Daniel Klein of George Mason University dismisses studies that ask professors whether they think of themselves as liberal or conservative, since the answers all depend on the frame of reference. They don't realize how liberal they are compared with the rest of the country. In addition, Klein suggests that professors often don't realize it when they bring their political biases into the classroom. "They just think they're teaching things the way they're reported in the *New York Times*." (We will leave the question of media bias for another book, but suffice it to say that the *New York Times* doesn't represent the political fifty-yard line for many Americans.)

The only place the authors of *Closed Minds* say they have seen a political shift on campus is in the natural sciences. Where the hard sciences have traditionally been more politically conservative than the social sciences and humanities, that difference has been disappearing.

When Seymour Martin Lipset and Everett C. Ladd Jr. wrote *The Divided Academy: Professors and Politics* in 1975, the gap between social and natural scientists was 19 percent in the 1968 election. Smith, Mayer, and Fritschler found that natural scientists were only 2 percent more likely to vote for the Republican candidate in the 2004 election. In other words, what little political variation there was on the university campus seems to be disappearing. (One explanation frequently offered by academic observers is that Republicans and conservatives have shown themselves to be "anti-science," and that debates over evolution and stem cells have shown scientists the true colors of the GOP. Another explanation is that science itself has become more politicized, with the addition of departments like "climate science" that have public policy at their heart rather than observational research.)

Klein and Charlotta Stern of the Swedish Institute for Social Research also found an even bigger gap than the authors of *Closed Minds* when they looked at the political leanings of social scientists and humanities professors. After examining actual voting records, they put the ratio of Democrats to Republicans at eight to one. Instead of offering "independent" as an option to their survey respondents, Klein and Stern asked to which party most of the candidates they've voted for recently have belonged. Everyone likes to be thought of as an independent, but when the rubber hits the road, pollsters tell us, there are very few genuine independents out there.

For the past few years a growing number of sociologists and political scientists have looked inward and asked how academia came to be so liberal. Is it a problem of selection—that is, are liberals the only ones who enter the ivory tower, and if so, why? Or do universities (either at the undergraduate, graduate, or professorial level) turn young men and women into liberals?

If you look at the theories offered about why liberals tend to be attracted to academia, they tend to fall into two categories. The first, to be blunt, is that liberals are smart, and smart people want to spend their time in an intellectual environment. As Jere Surber, a professor of philosophy at the University of Denver, wrote in the *Chronicle of Higher Education*, conservatives don't really understand the trajectory of history, and they don't understand that they are on the wrong side of it. Liberal arts professors, he writes "are liberal by deliberate and reasoned choice based on the best available evidence."

The second set of explanations comes from scholars who see the liberal leanings of professors as simply inevitable, based on their other characteristics. Neil Gross, a professor of sociology at the University of British Columbia, and Ethan Fosse, a doctoral candidate in sociology at Harvard, found that 43 percent of the political gap can be explained because college professors are more likely to have certain traits that are more often found among liberals. For instance, a disproportionate number of professors are Jewish or nonreligious. Those groups tend to be more liberal.

Matthew Woessner of Penn State, Harrisburg, and his wife April Kelly-Woessner, of Elizabethtown College, made a fascinating contribution to this discussion with a paper called "Left Pipeline: Why Conservatives Don't Get Doctorates" for the American Enterprise Institute. In it they hypothesized that the bulk of the ideological imbalance in academia is the result of differing personality traits. The scholars selected four traits—the importance placed on raising a family, making money, contributing original work to a particular field, and developing a meaningful philosophy of life—and matched them up with students' political self-definitions. "Ideology," they write, "represents far more than a collection of abstract political values." Liberalism, they found, "is more closely associated with a desire for excitement, an interest in creative outlets, and an aversion to a structured work environment. Conservatives express far greater interest in financial success and stronger desires to raise families." Then the researchers tried to figure out why people with those traits would or would not be attracted to academia.

Each side of the political spectrum will find something smugly satisfying in the study's portrayal of the other. ("Aha! I knew Republicans cared only about the rich," or "Show me someone who doesn't like a 'structured work environment' and I'll show you someone on the unemployment line.") There may be a kernel of truth to such generalizations. What is less obvious is why someone who places more importance on raising a family (a conservative) would shy away from academia.

When I interviewed her after the study was published, April Kelly-Woessner complained of sixty-hour work weeks she has had to endure as an academic. "And unlike a regular job, where you come home at five," she told me, "we're grading well into the evening."

Of course, those statements characterize most of the "regular jobs" that academics would have pursued if they weren't academics. From journalism to investment banking, it's hard to imagine a profession now that doesn't require so much time. Modern technology means that the professionals who don't have to log on and do some work at night are the exception. There are ways to work these hours around children's schedules.

In response to "Left Pipeline," Ilya Somin, a professor of law at George Mason University, wrote on the *Volokh Conspiracy* blog, "Relative to other professional jobs, academic careers are quite family friendly. Unlike most other professionals, professors have a high degree of control over their schedules [and] can do a higher proportion of their work at home."

Before beginning the research on this book, I agreed with Somin. And to some degree I still think that academia is a family-friendly profession. For those at the top of the ladder, anyway, it has become even more family-friendly than it was in the 1970s when my academic parents were raising me. In addition to a flexible schedule and long vacations, semesters have shortened, course loads have lightened, and salaries have risen.

But that's not the end of it. While those schedules are available for tenured professors, the rest of academia is a different story. The real problem for aspiring academics who want to raise families is being at the bottom of the ladder (particularly the increasing numbers who are stuck there permanently). Thanks in part to the institution of tenure (which the Woessners have both been granted), people just starting their families have very little in the way of job security. They are either graduate students, adjunct professors, or just starting the long road to tenure. They may have to take low-paying positions at multiple institutions; those positions may interfere with the completion of a dissertation, and they spend many of those early years engaged in a rush to publish a pile of articles and books. If you are a twenty-five-year-old with a strong ideological commitment to raising a family, the ivory tower may not be for you.

Some of the research discussed here may shed light on the "pool problem," the question of who goes into academia, but it does not explain entirely why academia *stays* so ideologically uniform. Fosse and Gross claim that one of the other characteristics found in disproportionately high numbers among academics is a tolerance for controversial ideas. One would think that more conservatives might be able to sneak into university life thanks to this characteristic. Or at least that more conservative ideas would sneak in.

But they haven't. Klein and Stern chalk this up to "groupthink," which they find prevalent in the academy. By groupthink they mean something very specific—not simply a bias toward a certain perspective, but the notion that there are "tendencies . . . toward concurrence-seeking, self-validation, and exclusion of challenges to core beliefs."

The first factor that Klein and Stern point to is "departmental majoritarianism," the notion that academic departments make most of the personnel decisions by vote and that only very rarely does an outsider override them. This system is the natural result of the narrow specialties of most academics, whose merit can allegedly be judged only by others in their field. Academic department members tend to seek out and attract people who are most like them, and they tend to reject those whom they consider misfits. In a 1988 paper, Queens University economist Lorne Carmichael argued that faculty must have tenure so that when they vote on a new member they will pick the best one, even if that person is more talented than the current members of the department. The older members must have confidence, according to Carmichael, that the younger ones won't take their positions.

Isn't this true for all types of organizations? To some extent, a corporate executive can hire people in his own image if he wants to, and then those people under him will do the same. More senior members might worry about hiring young persons who will take their jobs. But there are three important differences in higher education.

First, of course, academics claim that universities provide welcome environments to "misfits" and that they're always looking for different types and diverse perspectives. So this kind of intellectual cloning is a little hypocritical. Second, the corporate boss is unlikely to stay at one company for his entire career. Other people will be brought in, and the culture will likely change over time.

Third and most important, tenure makes this movement toward "consensus" long and almost irreversible. If you are a job candidate and you begin your career with some right-leaning tendencies, what is the likelihood you will keep them over time? The tenure process is a socialization process. People who can't learn to fit in often leave. And who can blame them? As Klein and Stern write, "Imagine building a career through graduate school and pre-tenure employment (about 11 years) just to be able to be yourself."

What would happen? They answer, "You find you are no longer yourself—not that your ideological views change much, but that any ideological *motivation* has likely receded. You go 'native' as they say. Your 20s and early 30s are a crucial period of development that cannot be reversed. Moreover, even after tenure you depend on department colleagues for pay raises, resources, teaching assignments, scheduling, promotions, recognition and consideration." The current system of academic hiring means that departments make all the decisions, and tenure raises the stakes of those decisions by making them permanent.

The other factor that seems to contribute to the groupthink mentality of university faculty is the lack of accountability built into the job market. Klein and Stern explain, "In all but the literal sense, one History department 'sells' its newly minted PhDs to other History departments. The consumers (History departments), the producers (other History departments) and the products (newly minted History PhDs) *are all historians.*" As noted earlier, this situation was purposefully created in the twentieth-century research university. Professors are experts, and only other experts in the field can judge the worth of the knowledge they produce.

Because administrators often come out of the same academic mold as professors, it's not unreasonable to think they would suffer from the same kinds of ideological rigidity as the rest of the university. In many cases they do. But they are, first of all, more likely answerable to students and parents and legislators and boards of trustees for their decisions. When there are complaints to be registered, administrators are on the front lines. On those occasions when they are allowed to meddle in the affairs of faculty, they are acting from a less insular perspective.

A dean's background may be in history, but he will occasionally have to make judgments about the curriculum, publication record, or teaching abilities of a professor in mathematics or biology.

Still, the institution of tenure largely ensures that administrators will be powerless. As Stephen Balch of the National Association of Scholars notes in a paper about "The Route to Academic Pluralism," "Tenure has the effect of creating a semi-permanent faculty, which, much like any other civil service, can delay, unravel, or roll back the efforts of transient reformers. Even with the best of wills, a university president contemplating a challenge to ideological vested interests must reckon on what can realistically be accomplished in the time he has available, together with the considerable damage the predictable hubbub will inevitably inflict on his subsequent advancement." Tenure is one of the things that gives faculty power over administrators. It is, in Balch's words, a "ring of intellectual defense" for the "status quo."

We have looked at some of the ways in which liberals may be more likely to become professors (for instance, because professors are disproportionately Jewish, and Jews are disproportionately liberal). We've also looked at how tenure may help keep universities liberal in the long run (by ensuring that people with the same ideas are hired, that there is little turnover on the faculty, and that administrators always lose battles of attrition over the future of the university).

But what if tenure itself is bringing a certain kind of person into the academic life? Harvard Professor Ruth Wisse wonders, "What sorts of people are attracted to university jobs because of the security they offer? Would there be a livelier, more entrepreneurial kind of teaching faculty if you did not have tenure? Is it self-selecting? Are the people who choose these jobs the kind of people who are leftists, who love the security of statism?"

For those who doubt the importance of tenure as a factor in getting people into university life, the anecdotal evidence bears review. For some professors, in fact, tenure seems to be one of the only things academia has going for it. Cathy Trower of Harvard conducted a survey trying to assess whether colleges could competitively recruit professors if they did not offer tenure. She found that while other factors could motivate a young academic's decision, like geography and work-life balance, tenure was almost always at the top of the wish list. Even a salary increase of 15 percent would not budge most of her respondents.

Here's what one graduate student told her: "It is not so much that we absolutely insist on security, but the reality is that academic life has so little going for it. There is only this one absolutely gratuitous benefit, which is that you have this absurd amount of security, which almost no one else in the workforce has. . . . The idea of setting it aside and all other elements of academic life remain moderately crappy . . . the way they are . . . that would seem like I just gave up a whole lot."

Carlin Romano, critic at large for the *Chronicle of Higher Education*, reports "the extraordinary degree to which you hear junior people worried about tenure." He believes there is a certain kind of "passivity" involved in the tenure system: "When you're on educational track, where every step is laid out, you just keep asking, 'Which hoop do you want me to jump through next?'" While Romano doesn't think tenure should be abolished altogether, he is bothered by "tenure's aspect of creating endlessly replicating series of people who place security in their lives above all else."

If, as the Woessners write, conservatives tend to care more about earning a higher salary, it doesn't mean they care more than liberals about compensation overall. After all, what tenure does is to offer professors a guaranteed income for a long time in return for giving up some amount of what they could be earning in another profession each year. Conservatives might just reject that tradeoff. For all the talk of professors being radical, it may be that conservatives value security less than liberals do. Maybe conservatives prefer being evaluated on the merit of what they contribute each year to their employer. Indeed, it's not only conservatives who may prefer such a system—Trower found that younger people today are generally more interested in being rewarded in this way than previous generations were.

But wait, critics will say, conservatives may not care about academic freedom, which is the real reason that liberals want tenure. Actually, Trower found in her survey that "the appeal of tenure was first and foremost about economic security and far less about academic freedom, although faculty wanted that too." In a real sense, whether you like tenure and whether you want to work in a university setting is in part based on how you prefer to be compensated for your efforts.

And when the Woessners report that conservatives tend to like a more "structured environment," it doesn't necessarily mean that conservatives like to be told what to do every hour of every day and as a result can't abide university life. Perhaps conservatives simply prefer to have clear sets of guidelines about what it takes to succeed in a profession. Instead, the tenure system may require that you learn to succeed in the popularity contest of a particular department, that you excel at "collegiality" (which is often an official consideration in the tenure process). The tenure process may simply be more subjective, more reliant on the uncontrolled whims of colleagues, than many people would like. In other words, there are good reasons not to go into a profession whose employment system is dominated by the tenure process.

If tenure is keeping the political identity of the university in place, there are also political forces that are keeping tenure in place. Interestingly, if a bit confusingly, those forces can be found on both the left and the right. Earlier, we saw how unionization is growing on college campuses across the country. Many collective bargaining units are trying to ensure that a certain percentage of faculty hired on each campus are either tenured or on the tenure track. Faculty unions are generally associated with national organizations like the NEA or the AFT, so they can wield power and influence policy far beyond their own campus. State legislators are generally loath to cross unions.

Add to this all the traditional academic organizations interested in keeping tenure, from the American Association of University Professors to the discipline associations like the Modern Language Association. Not surprisingly, most organizations that represent faculty are strongly in favor of the tenure system. And it's not only self-interest that's driving them. The AAUP's concerns about academic freedom are surely genuine.

For that matter, so are those at the Foundation for Individual Rights in Education. Although FIRE offers to defend all faculty from unnecessary abridgments of their freedoms, it often falls to them to defend libertarians and conservatives most. The leaders of FIRE believe that tenure serves as a bulwark, protecting what little intellectual diversity exists in the academy. As the president of FIRE, Greg Lukianoff, wrote in the *Los Angeles Times*, "Tenure serves a crucial function in higher education. Once earned (and it is not easy to do so), tenure allows accomplished professors to freely pursue their fields of study and even criticize the campus administration without fear of official reprisal. Without tenure, one can imagine the intellectual purges that would have taken place during American academic history as one fashionable idea gave way to another."

Somehow, though, tenure has produced the worst of both worlds. Lukianoff is right: American academic history in the twentieth century has largely been the story of "one fashionable idea giving way to another." In the quest for tenure, PhDs are always looking for the next hot trend. In the social sciences and humanities, close reading gave way to the new historicism, women's studies gave way to gender studies, black studies gave way to ethnic studies, and so on. At the same time tenure has promoted a certain kind of intellectual staleness. Many of the ideas were mediocre when they started at the top of the academic food chain, and by the time they reached the bottom, decades later, they were ut-terly devoid of any intellectual depth. These ideas take so long to work their way out of the academic system because of tenure.

In April 2009, the *Washington Post* asked a group of intellectuals and public figures what they would like to get rid of for "spring clean-ing." Francis Fukuyama, a tenured professor at Johns Hopkins, chose "tenure." In an interview he told me, "Every generation has a different approach to how you do molecular biology or political science. There is a natural cycle of generational change. The tenure system slows that down." He cites, for instance, in his own discipline of political science, the persistence of "rational choice theory," which has been around for a few decades now. And still, Fukuyama notes, "Outside of the academy no one cares about it."

The problems created by tenure, though, know no political boundar-ies. Fukuyama emphasizes, "Tenure is not a left-right thing. It protects incumbents regardless."

As it turns out, some conservatives in the academy have been mak-ing some serious, though small, inroads in liberal dominance in recent years. Professors like Robert George, director of the James Madison Program in American Ideals and Institutions at Princeton University, or Patrick Deneen, director of the Tocqueville Forum on the Roots of American Democracy at Georgetown University, not only have tenure, but they have also planted flags at their universities, and, with the help of a few donors, found a way to bring other young scholars into their orbits.

This is good news for intellectual diversity in higher education. But as it happens, then, conservatives too become "incumbents." And since their own ideologies run so contrary to the general tone of the univer-sity, they want the protections of tenure as much, if not more, than their liberal colleagues. Harvey Mansfield, Stephan Thernstrom, Paul Cantor, Harvey Silverglate, even my own father, David Schaefer—these are just a few of the conservative professors who have told me they support the institution of tenure.

These are professors who regularly say things that make administrators and other faculty members unhappy. They believe there is a good chance they would have been fired by now, were it not for tenure. I can't say they're wrong. But the question is whether their concerns should be outweighed by all the problems that tenure produces. The answer depends on which conservatives you ask.

Whatever the media and other academics might think, the right is not monolithic on the subject of higher education. While there is general agreement that many colleges and universities have gone off the deep end in the content of their teaching, the issue of how to reform them is one of spirited debate. Broadly speaking, there is a more populist strain of thinking, one that is represented by David Horowitz, for instance, who has pushed for an "Academic Bill of Rights." He wants to get more conservatives on campus through a sort of affirmative action program, countering one form of political ideology with another. A number of Republican politicians fall into Horowitz's camp. They are tired of how "out of touch" higher education is with the real world. They want colleges, particularly public ones, to be held more accountable to parents and taxpayers. Public universities should be contributing to the economy. They should be training people for jobs. Their ranks should not be filled with the likes of America-hating radicals like Ward Churchill.

The other strain on the right agrees that colleges should not be filled with Ward Churchills, but not because of Ward Churchill's politics per se. Rather, they see a lack of intellectual depth in the work of Churchill and his liberal colleagues. This strain on the right cares less about whether students read Ronald Reagan's speeches along with the "Communist propaganda" they are being assigned. They want to see a return to the classics—even if studying them will not put students "more in touch with the real world." *The Closing of the American Mind* is the rallying cry for these conservative intellectuals. And it's hard to imagine its author, Allan Bloom, making the case that universities should be contributing more to the local economy or that their faculties should be brought before state legislatures to account for the content of their curricula. (The divide is not always neat, but if you want to know on which side of it a conservative falls, ask his opinion on Sarah Palin.)

Until recently, the calls to end tenure came from the populist right. But there are good reasons it should come from the intellectual right as well. In addition to Fukuyama's point that tenure produces stagnation in areas where new thinking is important, it also pushes scholars further away from the classic texts by forcing them to constantly publish new theories rather than teach age-old truths to their students.

If these higher considerations won't convince the intellectual right to abandon tenure, maybe they will heed the words of Chester Finn, who now directs the Thomas B. Fordham Foundation. He does not think universities would simply get rid of all the conservatives on campus if tenure were not in place. But he does believe that conservatives "will stay an endangered species because of the academic culture."

He explains his own admittedly blunt calculus: "Protecting 411 conservatives is insufficient reason to retain a tenure system. Because it's protecting 400,000 liberals, too."

Just as there are forces on the left and the right with an interest in keeping tenure, so it's possible to see a bipartisan alliance, of sorts, to dispose of it. I was fairly convinced that no one involved with unions would ever question the worth of tenure. But then I met Richard Boris, director of the National Center for the Study of Collective Bargaining in Higher Education. A professor of political science at CUNY, Boris has a certain nostalgia for higher education in the mid-twentieth century. He clearly thinks the students then were more hardworking and the professors were held to a higher standard. "Tenure," he tells me, "is a problem." He thinks that changing it will not solve all the problems of higher education, but "tenure has to be on the table."

Boris largely dismisses claims that tenure is necessary to protect academic freedom. "At the end of the day it's about seniority," he tells me, adding, "but seniority can fuck up the system." Still, it's not clear what Boris is hoping for. He says that faculty "have to feel safe." He compares their jobs to working for the *Wall Street Journal*: "You have to feel that if you say something he doesn't like, Rupert Murdoch won't slit your throat the next day." Well, no, actually journalists don't have that kind of job protection. It's true that editors usually prevent reporters from putting things in the paper that would upset a paper's owner. But if something does sneak in, reporters don't have an equivalent of tenure that will keep them on the staff.

Boris is something of an outlier among union activists, to say the least. But I mention his perspective because throughout the interviews for this book, I have been surprised at who is willing to question tenure and who is not.

The institutions that have rejected tenure also represent a broad political cross section. Military schools and religious institutions are places where tenure is least prevalent. Of the hundred or so schools that are members of the Council for Christian Colleges and Universities, an evangelical group, about a third do not offer tenure. In an article published in the journal *Christian Higher Education*, the scholars Scott Harris of Plano Christian Academy and D. Barry Lumbsden of the University of Alabama surveyed the reasons why these schools did not offer tenure. The authors speculated that, for one thing, "term appointment may provide schools with a sense of control over confessional orthodoxy among their faculty members."

Critics will say that religious institutions don't have tenure because they don't care much about academic freedom. Certainly there have been outcries over the years when a professor is fired from a religious school for running afoul of its religious identity. When Joshua Hochschild was asked to leave the evangelical Wheaton College in 2006 after converting to Catholicism, for instance, the event merited a front-page story in the *Wall Street Journal*. In some of these cases, by the way, professors actually had tenure—like Tom Howard, who was asked to leave the evangelical Gordon College in 1993 for the same reason as Hochschild. But realistically, these cases are very few and extremely far between.

While researching my book *God on the Quad*, I found that religious colleges are not out to fire professors, just like they are not trying to kick out students. Contrary to what you read in some newspapers and magazines, the administrations are not engaged in an unending game of "gotcha" along theological lines. If anything, not having tenure forces them to be much more clear about their mission up front when they are hiring faculty.

Take Grove City College in Ohio, for instance. Its mission—religious, though nonsectarian—is to "to provide liberal and professional education of the highest quality that is within the reach of families with modest means who desire a college that will strengthen their children's spiritual and moral character." Professors at Grove City operate on a system of one-year contracts. They are evaluated by other faculty members, their students, and the administration.

The school has been on the AAUP's list of censured administrations for longer than any other, in a case dating back to 1962 when a professor named Larry Gara was fired for what the school deemed incompetence but for what Gara claimed were ideological reasons related to his objections to the Vietnam War. Sorting out the details of this case more than four decades later is a bit of a fool's errand, but it's safe to say that things ended happily for all involved. Gara went on to a forty-year career at Wilmington College in Ohio, from which he earned an honorary degree a couple of years ago. Wilmington College, according to its website, "leads students to gain an awareness of the world, to acquire knowledge of career and vocation, and to seek truth and social justice." In other words, Gara ended up at a school whose vision of higher education he shared.

What's interesting about Gara's case, though, is its uniqueness in Grove City's history. Since 2000, the school has hired fifty-six faculty members. Only one of those was dismissed, and that was for failing to make sufficient progress on a dissertation. "The faculty who come here are not under any illusions about the things we want them to do," says the dean, John Sparks.

Nor, for instance, are the faculty at Hampshire College in Massachusetts, which also has a distinctly clear mission. Hampshire has no traditional majors, and students don't receive grades. Since its founding in 1958, it has encouraged its students to be politically engaged. And it also doesn't offer tenure. The idea is that the school always wants to be on the cutting edge.

As Ralph Hexter, Hampshire's president explains, "The founders envisioned a teaching force that would be recent graduates of top PhD programs. They would teach and explore in this very open student curriculum and then move on to other jobs." Hexter tells me, "We were very interdisciplinary from the beginning. There was a sense that they wanted a fairly flexible faculty who could be presenting the latest things to students. This was not supposed to be a place where things would settle into certain ways and be fixed for decades."

The founders wanted young faculty with radical ideas to come and teach for a few years on their way to something else. It hasn't worked out that way, in part because there are no other jobs for them to move on *to*. Still, a vestige of the founding ideas remain—tenure still isn't a part of the school's promotion system. New faculty are granted a three-year contract, then a four-year contract, and then contracts in ten-year increments after that. Hampshire doesn't fire many people either.

Better-known Bennington College also has not historically offered tenure, though over the years a kind of "presumptive tenure" system has developed, with faculty receiving five-year reviews. In 1994, though, the board of trustees decided to return to its original situation with no tenure. Twenty-five professors were let go. In part, the considerations were financial—the school's enrollment and endowment were falling fast, and something had to be done. In its Symposium Report from that year, the board wrote, "Under the new system, faculty experimentation and innovation will be invited and rewarded; the faculty member and the institution make explicit commitments to each other relating the faculty member's plans and performance to those of the College as a whole."

Again, like it or not, Bennington's mission should leave faculty in no doubt about what they are getting into. Each year, this statement is read at the school's commencement: "Bennington regards education as a sensual and ethical, no less than an intellectual process. It seeks to liberate and nurture the individuality, the creative intelligence, and the ethical and aesthetic sensibility of the students, to the end that their richly varied natural endowments will be directed toward self-fulfillment and toward constructive social purposes." With no majors, no official curriculum, and the presence of practicing artists and poets on campus, Bennington is still trying to be the avant-garde institution its founders envisioned.

Carlin Romano thought he fit this model. He was a "practitioner"— that is, he was the book critic for the *Philadelphia Inquirer* at the time he took a job as a philosophy professor at Bennington, a few years after the twenty-five were let go. "The lack of tenure didn't scare me off. I have never been a particularly security-minded person," he tells me. He enjoyed his time at Bennington, but things did not end well. The president of the college, Elizabeth Coleman, did not renew the contract of one of the school's theater professors. Romano, who thought the professor was being unduly punished for personal reasons, went to the board of trustees to complain and demanded the president's resignation. Romano was subsequently fired as well.

Romano does worry that in the absence of tenure, a college president could gain too much power, as he believes has happened at Bennington. "The lack of tenure means a lack of protection for professors who get on the bad personal side of an executive." Still, Romano always had his job at the *Inquirer*, so he wasn't risking as much in his confrontation as a faculty member who depended on a school for his entire salary. Since then, Romano has left the *Inquirer*; in the fall of 2010 he was set to take another teaching job at Ursinus College. He seemed not the least concerned that once again he would not have tenure.

There are other "practitioners," like Romano, who remain largely uninterested in tenure. Webster University in St. Louis offered professors the choice between tenure and more frequent leaves to do faculty development. Although many of its faculty are practitioners, and so are not necessarily wedded to the idea of a permanent academic career, it is nonetheless surprising that two-thirds of the senior faculty have given up tenure for continuing status contracts (that are renewed every five years).

West Point's administration would probably not describe itself in the terms that Bennington or Hampshire does, though it values having some turnover in its faculty. The school has a steady stream of younger faculty who come in for two- or three-year appointments. As Bruce Keith, associate dean of academic affairs, explains, it's important for the school to have people with "field experience, who come in and can talk about the West Point curriculum with cadets and explain how it may be applied in the field."

Four of the five service academies do not have formal tenure for their faculties. Senior military faculty have a mandatory retirement age—often before they are sixty years old. So tenure wouldn't make much sense for them. Senior civilian faculty are offered long-term contracts for their service.

The AAUP has periodically worried about the lack of tenure at the service academies. It issued a report on West Point after Congress voted to significantly increase the civilian faculty on campus—but there have been few problems. A procedure at West Point allows faculty to register complaints about violations of their academic freedom. But in the fifteen years Keith has been at the school, not a single faculty member has even initiated the procedure.

What do these schools—religious, military, radical, conservative—have in common? Why have they all determined they can do without tenure? The answer is this: these institutions have strong and clear missions. Few professors would even apply to these schools if they did not believe fully in the schools' missions.

This kind of transparency from a college administration is hard to find these days. As Stanley Fish writes in *Save the World on Your Own Time*, "Pick up the mission statement of almost any college or university, and you will find claims and ambitions that will lead you to think that it is the job of an institution of higher learning to cure every ill the world has ever known: not only illiteracy and cultural ignorance, which are at least in the ball-park, but poverty, war, racism, gender bias . . . and the hegemony of Wal-Mart." Reading such a call to arms, in other words, a professor could be forgiven for being confused as to exactly what his bosses want from him.

Elizabeth Samet, an English professor at West Point, reflects on her decision to apply for a job at the military school in her recent book, *A Soldier's Heart*. She recalls the ad in the Modern Language Association's job information list to which she responded. Applicants should have a "genuine concern for the development of competent and committed military officers." She reflects on her own decision to apply for the job: "Curious as I was, I knew that West Point's priorities and protocols were not those to which I had grown accustomed. It was, after all, a school that trained men and women in the use of the M-16 rifle, the M-203 grenade launcher, and the M-249 machine gun even as it educated them in foreign languages, mathematics, and literature." (Even in higher education, it turns out that guns make matters much clearer.) Only after serious consideration did Samet take a position there.

West Point has also put in place some very clear policies and annual reviews so that faculty know what is expected of them. There are five areas of excellence—teaching, publishing, service, faculty development, and student development—which each faculty member is supposed to aim for. They are even asked each year whether they understand these requirements and whether they think they can fulfill them. According to Keith, some faculty say they may not be able to accomplish all they are supposed to. But the vast majority always report that they understand what is being asked of them.

The kind of reflection Samet engaged in before applying for a job at West Point should be the kind of reflection that every professor goes through. Do I understand what this school is doing? Do I belong at this school? Do I believe in this school's mission? Will I be fulfilling it?

While administrators are often at fault for failing to define that mission, faculty rarely press them to clarify. Instead they apply for jobs at any school that is hiring and hope to hit the tenure jackpot, at which point they can go about their career without much regard for institutional mission. Of course, the state of the job market doesn't help matters either.

But if tenure weren't on the table, if the academic life didn't seem to go hand in hand with lifetime job security, professors would be more likely to ask themselves these questions. And students might begin to reap the benefits.

# 7

# Following the Money

If colleges were to eliminate tenure tomorrow, they'd have to pay faculty higher salaries. That's what most economists—and common sense—will tell you. Lifetime job security is a perk, like health insurance or a company car. If you take it away, you'll have to compensate in another way to get the same quality of employees.

Tenure means not having to worry about having to find new employment in middle age, and that means a lot to professors. As George Mason University economist Tyler Cowen explains, "In a lot of academia, once you're over fifty it's hard to get another job, even if you've done well." He compares it to being a computer programmer, where age seems to be a disadvantage no matter how talented you are. Taking an academic job without the promise of tenure is what Cowen calls "a massive risk." So there would have to be a lot of money on the front end to make up for it.

In the long term, though, the costs might even out. Higher education would have a more sensible-looking labor market in which colleges could ensure that all the faculty members were pulling their weight. This is particularly important for small colleges, says Bruce Johnstone, who has served as president of the University of Buffalo and a vice president at the University of Pennsylvania. Large universities, in his experience, "tend to have ways of cushioning the existing departmental configurations a bit better than community colleges or small private colleges." Johnstone, who has also been a trustee at a Catholic college, says that smaller schools "need to add and subtract programs much faster and therefore need to be freer of the constraints of tenure."

In areas of study that were not attracting many students, colleges could eliminate departments or form consortia with other area schools so that no one was paying the salaries of full tenured professors to teach handfuls of students. Colleges could spend much less money subsidizing the kind of trivial research and publication that have become the central focus of the tenure process and spend more money to support good teaching.

They could also spend more of their salary budgets on younger faculty, bringing some fresh blood into the community. Shirley Tilghman, president of Princeton University, confesses that her biggest concern about the current economic downturn is that universities will miss out on recruiting a new generation of faculty. Tilghman, who in the past has expressed her reservations about tenure's disproportionately negative effects on women, says, "The thing that will have the longest-term negative impact on colleges and universities is if we can't figure out how to continue the careers of young people just coming out of grad school. We have a demographic problem," she adds, with such a high percentage of the faculty coming from the Boomer generation. She believes it will be "devastating for universities if we go through a four-to-five-year period of hiring freezes."

Without tenure, all faculty could be hired instead on five-year renewable contracts—perhaps shorter ones earlier in their career and longer ones later, after they have proven themselves. The greater flexibility provided by this system might allow colleges to use fewer adjunct professors, thereby improving the quality of the education students receive. And professors might also be willing to give up some compensation in return for flexibility. As Stephen Prothero, professor of religion at Boston University, says, "It would be so much different if there were a free and open labor market. People wouldn't be stuck for life in all kinds of cities they don't want to live in." One reason why middle-aged people in academia have such a difficult time getting a job is that there are almost no job openings, let alone senior job openings. People get tenure, and then they get "stuck."

Even if contracting for faculty might cost slightly more in the long term, many colleges would be willing to make the investment if they knew they weren't locked into funding a particular position for the next four decades.

If a group of universities in the same tier decided together to eliminate tenure, the economic effects on any one university might be minimal, particularly if those schools were at the top of the education food chain. Harvard wouldn't have to pay a professor any more to compete with Yale if Yale had eliminated tenure as well.

But if one school were to go out on a limb and eliminate tenure, it would surely have to pay significantly higher salaries when recruiting new professors. On the other hand, that school's leaders might also find that low-quality faculty were more likely to jump ship, knowing that an end to their careers there might be close at hand. That university might have stumbled on a useful market signal—telling professors that they shouldn't come unless they are sure of their own talent and their own commitment to the university. In other words, they would accomplish what schools like Grove City, West Point, and Hampshire have done— set out a clear mission for the school and clear terms of employment.

In at least one way, tenure as a perk is different from health insurance or a company car. The people most likely to have tenure are those who are least likely to need it. The star professors out there—Stanley Fish, Henry Louis Gates, Alan Dershowitz, and many others that no one outside academia has ever heard of—do not need tenure. They are lured from one university to the next by higher salaries, better jobs for their spouses, more temperate climates, and other baubles. They operate in a market that looks much like the corporate world. Colleges continue to shell out more money for these professors because tenure never even enters into their calculations. But no one knows whether the kind of flexibility that has developed at the top of the higher-education ladder could be replicated lower down.

Ed Larson, a Pulitzer Prize–winning professor of history at Pepperdine University, who served as associate counsel for the House Committee on Education and Labor, compares higher education to baseball. Getting rid of tenure, he says, would be akin to introducing free agency into the major leagues. It brought a lot more flexibility to team managers and players, but it also made things much more expensive. Free agency in baseball came about when the reserve clause—which tied players to a particular team even after their contract had been fulfilled—was thrown out by an arbitrator. Interestingly, the reserve clause, which smacks of academic tenure, was opposed by the players, who thought they could get a better deal as free agents. The "players" in academia haven't yet come around to that view of tenure.

Still, eliminating tenure could produce results we can't predict. "Tenure affects the very nature of higher education," says Larson. "Removing it would be like changing the pitching mound or the distance to the bases."

If removing tenure is unlikely to improve the bottom line at most colleges, why should we consider it now? After all, colleges are in dire financial straits. What they need is a plan for making education more affordable, not less so. If the net economic effect of tenure is unknown at best, and a financial disadvantage at worst, why should we encourage colleges to eliminate it?

For just the reason that Larson elucidates. Higher education is so broken right now that it's time to change the pitching mound and the distance to the bases—not to mention the strike zone and the number of players on each team. Before we do that, though, we need to look at the big picture.

In his 2008 book *Economic Facts and Fallacies*, Stanford economist Thomas Sowell cuts to the heart of the problem with the higher-education market. "In ordinary commercial transactions, for the seller's interest to completely override the buyer's interest would be to risk losing that customer to someone else. But in academia," Sowell argues, "almost by definition the student does not fully understand the nature of the product being sold. If a student already understood the content of a course, there would be no point in taking that course."

It's easy to mock the notion that college professors know so much more than the rest of us—so much that we couldn't possibly understand how valuable they are. But Sowell is right: there is a fundamental imbalance of information in the purchase of a college education (unless one's parents are academics, and even then they will not be experts in every field their child wishes to take a class in).

But it's not simply that students can't fathom the worth of a course before they have taken it. It's also that students and parents typically value higher education for reasons that are different from professors' reasons. As Burt Weisbrod, a professor of economics at Northwestern University, notes, it's hard to settle on an understanding of what a quality college education looks like when the "buyers" and "sellers" have such different understandings of it. "For parents, by and large, their orientation is pretty clearly and overwhelmingly toward job opportunities," Weisbrod says. "They want their kids to be able to make a good living after graduation." But, he observes, "If you talk to faculty, especially at the undergrad level, they don't think that's their function. It's not that students' job prospects are irrelevant," just that he and his colleagues "see [themselves] as helping people be curious about life, curious about world, and thoughtful about alternatives."

In some other economic transactions the buyer and seller have different understandings of the product. Suppose I start a newspaper tomorrow. I might think I'm selling excellent journalism while my "readers" are actually using my product to line their birdcages. It might work out fine. But the imbalance in this transaction does make it difficult to talk in general terms about making the product better, or whether the product is worth what I'm charging for it. I might think I should improve my grammar. My customers might want me to make the paper thicker.

Despite these misgivings, the interests of the buyers and sellers in higher education do seem to align fairly well in some respects. Students and parents who are most interested in post-graduation job prospects and long-term salary potential tend to judge institutions by their reputations. They assume that an employer who sees a well-known school on a résumé will place that résumé on the top of the pile. Which may be true.

As explored earlier, it means that parents will tend to value faculty research (though they may not realize it) over teaching when choosing a college, because it's the research that forms an institution's reputation. Even at the lower-tiered schools, parents and students who are choosing among different options will want the one with the best reputation. And even at the lower-tiered "teaching" schools, reputation is still determined by research output.

For most faculty, that system has worked well. While they may say they think higher education is important because it teaches students to be curious about the world, professors also care about their own success. Since it is usually research productivity that leads to tenure, professors are just fine with parents judging a school by its reputation.

But some evidence suggests that the current alignment of interests between buyers and sellers is starting to fall apart. Findings have shown for a long time that it doesn't matter what college a student attends. One study revealed that students who got into Ivy League schools but decided to go to less prestigious colleges did just as well financially as their peers from the Ivy League. But now that fewer students are getting the jobs they want—or any jobs—coming out of even the top colleges, parents may begin to question seriously the value of higher education.

In fact, if we are to believe the headlines, the market for higher education is on the verge of collapse. As Mark Taylor, a Columbia professor
of religion, recently wrote in his book *Crisis on Campus*, "The education
bubble is about to burst. There are disturbing similarities between the
dilemma colleges and universities have created for themselves and the
conditions that led to the collapse of major financial institutions supposedly too secure to fail. The value of college and university assets (i.e.,
endowments) has plummeted. The schools are overleveraged, liabilities
(debts) are increasing, liquidity is drying up, fixed costs continue to
climb, their product is increasingly unaffordable and of questionable
value in the marketplace, and income is declining."

Taylor's comparison of higher education to the financial industry is
common these days. And his "bubble" assessment is not far off, at least
for the time being. Harvard now has $5 billion in debt. Dartmouth lost
its triple-A bond rating. State governments are cutting back, but colleges
and parents are still hoping that the federal government will bail them
out by increasing student aid and research grants. Meanwhile, states are
raising tuition by leaps and bounds. The price for a year at the University of California rose by a third in 2010, from $7,788 to $10,302. With
another $14,000 or so for room and board, the annual cost for a Cali-
fornia resident to attend UC will exceed $24,000 in 2011. For students
attending a public university, that price tag has been quite a shock.

Tenure is not the primary cause of the financial problems described
by Taylor and others. The long-term fixed costs of tenured professors
are not the main reason tuitions are going up. The faculty have not
been responsible for making the bad investments that have sunk college
endowments (though at public universities senior faculty pensions are
certainly taking a toll on long-term budgets).

But tenure is one reason why colleges will have such a difficult time
digging themselves out of the current mess. Tenure shifts the balance
of power on campus in favor of the faculty. Unfortunately, the tenured
faculty are among the least concerned with an institution's bottom line.

They can be fired only in a total financial emergency. And they rarely hear about students' or parents' dissatisfaction with the education they are providing or the sticker price for a year of college. As counterintuitive as it sounds, administrators, who tend to have much less power than faculty, are the ones out on the sales floor while the faculty are in the back offices making the major decisions.

In the sections that follow, we'll look at the larger picture of the economics of higher education in order to understand the place of tenure in this problem. We need to understand how colleges and universities came to be in such desperate straits, and to sort out the interests of all the parties involved in the transaction if we expect to fix them.

What has led to the current economic plight of the universities? In their recent book, *Higher Education?*, CUNY history professor Andrew Hacker and *New York Times* reporter Claudia Dreifus walk through some of the numbers. "The big-ticket item at most colleges is faculty salaries, especially at tenured levels," they write. In fact, it's surprising that salaries don't make up more of the cost.

According to a report from the Delta Project on Postsecondary Education Costs, Productivity, and Accountability (whose mission is to help improve college affordability by controlling costs and improving productivity), the share of spending on instruction (which "includes faculty salaries and benefits, office supplies, administration of academic departments, and the proportion of faculty salaries going to departmental research and public service") declined between 1998 and 2008. At public research institutions, spending on instruction went from 62.8 percent to 61.7 percent of the budget. But again, faculty salaries were only one part of that. At private bachelor's-degree-granting institutions, spending on instruction (which included all of those other elements besides faculty salaries) dropped from 39.9 percent to 38.9 percent during that period. The data "show that the common myth that spending on faculty is responsible for continuing cost escalation is not true," according to the authors of the study.

It's easy, though, to understand the outrage felt by Hacker, Dreifus, and numerous other observers of higher education. Describing a particular salary in the six figures for an "*annual* teaching schedule of 130 hours," Hacker and Dreifus are justified in getting a little punchy. They write, "Say good-bye to Mr. Chips with his tattered tweed jacket; today's senior professors can afford Marc Jacobs."

The average salary of full-time professors has gone up, certainly. Adjusted for inflation, faculty salaries increased every one of the last ten years until 2010 (when they increased more slowly than the rate of inflation). Faculty who taught at the same university from 2007 to 2008 saw their salaries increase 4.6 percent after inflation in that year. But the boom times were especially good to big-name universities. Rich schools got much, much richer. Hacker and Dreifus point to faculty at Duke University, for instance, where faculty salaries have risen 65 percent in constant dollars since the 1980s.

"Why have faculty salaries increased so markedly?" they ask. Their answer—"The money has been there"—is not satisfying. Hacker and Dreifus suggest that parents associate prestige with higher salaries and so were willing to pay the higher tuition fees to compensate professors more. Possibly. But do parents know the salaries of the faculty teaching their kids? And just because there is money available, should it automatically be allocated to faculty? There are plenty of other ways to throw around cash at a university.

When people ask Burt Weisbrod—who coauthored a book called *Mission and Money: Understanding the University*—why tuition has risen so much in recent years, he tells them, "You ain't seen nothing yet." Weisbrod argues that, given the model for higher education, colleges and universities have actually managed to keep their instructional costs down remarkably well.

Higher education is labor intensive. Teaching hasn't changed much in the past thousand years. One person stands up in front of a room, and other people listen. Whereas other sectors of the economy have experienced important new efficiencies by substituting capital for labor—thanks to modern machinery, we don't need as many hours of labor now to put together a car or build a house—this has not happened in higher education. Other sectors of the economy continue to drive up the cost of skilled labor, but higher education—at least as it has been traditionally structured—can't keep up. Men and women with college and graduate degrees can be gainfully employed and well compensated by corporations, hospitals, law firms, and technology companies.

Weisbrod suggests that colleges have found ways to keep spending on instruction relatively stable despite the fact that the cost of labor has gone up significantly. For instance, average class sizes have multiplied, he says, sometimes by ten or fifteen times since the mid-twentieth century. According to the Delta Cost Project, enrollment has increased nearly 26 percent from 1998 to 2008 alone, with the full-time undergraduate population rising the most. But the number of faculty has not grown correspondingly.

"The faculty cost per student is way down," Weisbrod says. But he wonders, "What is that doing to the quality of education? We believe by and large that these bigger classes are less effective at teaching students." You can find a mix of opinions on this question of how class size has affected quality. Bruce Johnstone, the distinguished university professor of higher and comparative education emeritus at the University of Buffalo, recalls his education at Harvard in the early 1960s: "When I was there, professors taught huge classes with fabulous graduate assistants, and they were brilliant. The professors didn't spend any time with students. I didn't expect them to." Johnstone said that his son, who attended Harvard a few years ago, had a lot of "smaller, odd courses," but ultimately "the teaching didn't get any better."

Of course, colleges have also saved money on instruction by hiring adjuncts and contingent faculty. Tenured faculty salaries may rise, even as tenured faculty refuse to teach large numbers of students. But adjuncts will take over large classes for as little as $2,000 a course. There is no sign that the supply of adjunct labor is falling, and despite the horrendous outlook for job prospects in academia, a surprisingly large number of college graduates choose this course each year.

Weisbrod compares higher education to health care, another labor-intensive sector of the economy. While health care has made great strides and uses a great deal of technology, people are still needed to decide who should have different tests and treatments, and to perform them. So health care has hired the equivalent of adjuncts—medical technicians—to lower some of its labor costs.

Consumers may object to the skyrocketing costs of health care or the large insurance company bureaucracies, but most Americans still recognize a difference between health care in 1960 and 2010. To start with, average life expectancy has increased by eight years or so. Some of this is due to advances in public health, but it is also the result of better drugs, advances in surgical procedures, smarter diagnostic tests, and so on. Which makes you wonder: what significant strides have been made in higher education that justify its growing costs? Do college graduates seem smarter or better prepared? Are they more curious about the world around them? Are they better-informed citizens?

Despite the significant reliance on adjuncts and larger class sizes, the cost to get one student an undergraduate education has gone up. The College Board reports that since 1982, tuition charges at private colleges have risen two and a half times in inflation-adjusted dollars. College tuition has risen faster than median family income, faster than car prices, even faster than—get this—prescription drugs.

Until recently, though, the pain of the tuition increases was cushioned by huge increases in financial aid. Tuition may have gone from about $10,000 to about $25,000 at private four-year colleges between 1980 and 2008, and from $2,500 to $6,000 at public colleges, but financial aid , on average rose, from $5,000 to $12,000. In other words, financial aid has risen at the same rate as tuition. This is not a coincidence. Colleges know they can continue to raise prices because someone other than their customers is picking up the tab. The third-party payer system has meant that consumers have been shielded from the increasing costs of higher education. So for all the outrage about the higher-education price tag, few families have had to opt out.

In 2008 and 2009 it was striking how many newspaper articles contained heartrending accounts of middle-class families choosing state schools for their children over private ones. Would this have been news in any other market? In a sector where the government *wasn't* paying for such a big percentage of the product, more people would have seriously considered lower-cost alternatives a long time ago.

When confronted with these headlines about skyrocketing tuition, college administrators like to say that parents and students are covering only a fraction of the actual cost of educating a student. But what does this mean? Some observers, as Thomas Sowell writes, "take this as a sign of the altruism of a non-profit institution." But it's not. Sowell explains, "Since teaching is one of the joint products of an academic institution, along with research and other ancillary activities, the meaning of such a statement is elusive." Why should tuition cover all the activities of the university? "No one would take seriously a similar statement made by the owner of the New York Yankees if he said that fans who go to Yankee Stadium do not pay the full cost of running a baseball team." That is, the fact that fans don't pay for every part of running a baseball team doesn't mean that the owners are just being generous by giving them tickets at such a "low" cost. Colleges get revenues from other sources to do things other than educate undergraduates.

As it turns out, students and parents *are* bearing an ever larger share of the costs of universities. According to the Delta Cost Project, "the student share of costs is rising primarily to replace institutional subsidies—and not to enable greater spending." This "cost-shifting," according to the authors, means that "while students are paying more, they are not necessarily getting more bang for their educational buck."

In fact, undergraduate tuition is often used to subsidize graduate education—so they may be getting less bang for the buck. Ohio University economist Richard Vedder estimates that schools spend anywhere from five to fifteen times as much on graduate students as on undergraduates. Grad students are taught in small classes with senior professors. And students in doctoral programs (as opposed to those who leave after taking a master's degree) are generally on some kind of fellowship. They pay no tuition and receive a school-year stipend of between $10,000 and $20,000. Colleges recoup some of the loss by putting grad students, rather than senior professors, in front of classrooms. But parents should still doubt the idea that colleges are somehow doing them a favor by educating their children.

Yet the costs incurred in educating each student have grown. The frills that universities have added are the easiest targets. Even when I was a Harvard student in the mid-1990s, I knew that the annual lobster dinner in the cafeteria was not what my parents had in mind when they wrote tuition checks. But things have only grown worse in the fifteen years since: state-of-the-art gym facilities, restaurant-quality cafeteria food, extracurricular activities to serve every interest. Posh dormitories are now the norm at four-year private schools and even many public universities. Wi-Fi is everywhere on campus and a number of schools even give iPods (soon it will no doubt be iPads) to freshmen, ostensibly so they can listen to lectures and practice foreign languages. News of the economic downturn brought many of the most absurd cases to light. Williams College announced it would cut back on free massages for students.

Vedder, director of the Center for College Affordability and Productivity, refers to this trend as "the country-clubization of the American university." Of the money spent by colleges on nonacademic pursuits, he told the *New York Times*, "A lot of it is for great athletic centers and spectacular student union buildings. In the zeal to get students, they are going after them on the basis of recreational amenities."

The great athletic departments, too, have long been a source of contention—an unnecessary expense even to the most casual observer.

While college administrations claim that the greater visibility provided by a high-level sports program brings in more money from alumni and from TV broadcasts, and even a larger number of applicants, the evidence suggests that spending on college athletics detracts from both a college's education and its bottom line. Colleges lose money and student athletes lose time spent in class while traveling around the country. And students and taxpayers increasingly foot the bill. According to a 2010 article in *USA Today*, "More than half of athletic departments at public schools in the Football Bowl Subdivision were subsidized by at least 26% last year, up from 20% in 2005. That's a jump of $198 million when adjusting for inflation and includes money from student fees, university support and state subsidies." When even a Division III school like Williams, with fewer than two thousand students on campus, has a $4 million athletics budget, it's clear that things have spun out of control.

The Knight Commission on Intercollegiate Athletics recently looked at spending on athletics in the Football Bowl Subdivision conferences. The commission found, for instance, that in the Southeastern Conference, the median athletic spending per athlete was more than ten times higher than the median spent on a student for education and related expenses. Even the Mid-America Conference—which is not exactly filled with athletic powerhouse schools—spent four times as much on athletes as on students.

The commission also found that between 2005 and 2008, spending (which included only operating expenses like coaches' salaries and team travel, not stadiums) rose almost 38 percent in constant dollars. Perhaps the most shocking part of all this is that we don't even compensate the athletes. With all that money being paid out, surely there's some left for the guys actually throwing, kicking, and hitting the balls.

If you were looking to cut a university's budget, athletics and other "extras" are the most obvious places to start. But Jane Wellman, executive director of the Delta Cost Project, says that they are not the primary reason for rising costs at most universities. At larger public universities, where most college students are enrolled, Wellman says it's important to look at the category of "academic support." This includes not only technology and libraries but also remedial education. The arguments for cutting back in these areas are less clear-cut than those for cutting out lobster dinners and gymnastics teams, but they are important to air.

Sure, we want our children to have access to state-of-the-art research facilities, but how important is that for an undergraduate education? If anything, one would think that the cost of library facilities should be going down with all the material that can now be found online. But the proliferation of journals, even ones online, and academic tomes has forced university library budgets to grow.

Who reads these? Undergraduates have long joked about how seldom they enter libraries during their time in school, but it is true that many university libraries seem to exist more for the benefit of the faculty and the graduate students. University librarians report that many of the journals to which their schools subscribe, and many of the university press books they buy, are rarely, if ever, read.

Technology is another area where colleges are spending more without examining the value added. About ten years ago, I walked into a classroom full of laptops for the first time. As I sat in the back, I noticed that few students were taking notes. Only a handful was paying attention to the professor at all. Everyone else was emailing, web surfing, or playing solitaire. Not much has changed since.

College classrooms are now routinely equipped with at least two computers and a complete audio visual set up. Every student in the room has a laptop open. The rooms all have Wi-Fi. But is any more learning going on? A dean at Southern Methodist University made news in the *Chronicle of Higher Education* when he decided to make classes low-tech again, removing these classroom computers. Professors, he argued, were relying too much on PowerPoint presentations for their teaching, and students were disengaging as a result. He has saved money not only on technology—the systems were getting old and would have needed to be replaced shortly—but also on support staff who were regularly called in to deal with glitches in the classroom computers.

A recent survey in a British education journal found that 59 percent of students found more than half their classes boring. And they found PowerPoint and other kinds of computer-assisted classroom activities particularly dull. Even "interactive" activities in computer labs were said to be less engaging than old-fashioned lectures and discussions. One needn't be a Luddite to conclude that cutting back on technology might have some positive effects.

The final segment of academic support that is responsible for rising costs is remedial education, whose price tag will continue to grow as our K–12 education system continues to decline. Despite a 3.29 grade point average in high school, nearly half the entering freshmen at California State University campuses in 2009 could not get into entry-level college English. Almost 40 percent could not get into entry-level math. All these students were sent first to remedial classes to brush up on what they should have learned in high school.

Remedial education, by definition, costs too much for colleges. Why are they paying people who are qualified to teach at the college level to offer courses that are part of the high school curriculum? Students who are not qualified to take beginning-level English and math in college shouldn't be admitted to four-year colleges, particularly those paid for by the public. (One might blame admissions officers to start. But imagine the public uproar when students who graduate with honors from California high schools are regularly rejected from the lower-tier state universities.) These students need a different kind of "gap year"—one in which they brush up on the knowledge they should have gotten in high school. This is the role that community colleges can best and most inexpensively fulfill.

With the growth of all these different segments of the university—technology, remedial education, sports, entertainment, food choices—

it's little wonder that college administrations have become so bloated. Between 2004 and 2007, the median number of senior administrators grew at public four-year schools by 1.8 percent annually and at private not-for-profit schools by 3.4 percent annually. As of 2007, private colleges employed one senior administrator for every thirty-five students.

In a 2009 article in *Forbes Magazine*, Daniel Bennett of the Center for College Affordability and Productivity wrote of the positions he found while perusing the *Chronicle of Higher Education's* classified section, "Georgia Southern University has an opening for a recreation therapist, the University of Florida an opening for a director of multicultural and diversity affairs, and the University of Maryland, College Park, openings for a coordinator of off-campus student involvement and a director of fraternity and sorority life." He asks, reasonably, "Will educational outcomes improve with the addition of positions such as these?" More important, in a time when everyone is cutting back, shouldn't these sorts of positions be the first to go?

Colleges, it should be said in their defense, don't always spend money on administrative positions of their own accord. The legal hoops that colleges must jump through have gotten higher and more numerous in recent years. Schools now employ compliance officers to help with reporting to the government everything from crime rates on campus to environmental safety to student finance data. Like all other large, wealthy institutions, colleges are routinely slapped with lawsuits. Universities are regularly sued over students' drinking, sexual harassment, and employment discrimination, among other matters. So universities employ people both to avoid such problems and also to defend themselves when necessary. Nevertheless, plenty of the administrative buildup by colleges is voluntary and wasteful. If you were looking to reduce costs, trimming the administration would be a good place to start.

Especially since most senior administrators are powerless to fix the things that are really broken.

What is most absurd about this new army of administrators is that they have almost no impact on reducing the faculty's wasteful and self-indulgent behaviors. Where is the administrator in charge of college facilities when a professor announces that his courses will be held only Tuesday through Thursday between the hours of 11 a.m. and 3 p.m.? According to a 2007 Faculty Senate Report, the provost of Stanford University himself complained "of the wastes of space" and "unused classrooms."

But most administrators, like the Stanford provost, have little power to do anything about such "waste." As Thomas Sowell explains, "The unique position of college and university faculty members as both labor and management offers many different kinds of opportunities to serve their own interests, rather than the interests of the students or of the academic institution." Even something as superficial as allowing professors to choose when to hold classes can have serious consequences for students. The fact that many classes are scheduled in the same small window often makes it harder for students to take all the classes they need for graduation in four years.

Limited amounts of time in the classroom—twelve hours a week for two fourteen-week semesters a year—"means that there is not enough learning going on," says Bruce Johnstone of the University of Buffalo. But eliminating all that "white space" will be almost impossible because of inflexible and powerful tenured faculties.

Johnstone says the academic schedule is only one part of the problem. He bemoans the incoherence of the undergraduate curriculum, and there too, he knows who is to blame: "There is too much allowing the faculty to decide what they teach and when they want to teach it." Too few classes have prerequisites. Students come into classes with varying levels of background knowledge, and professors usually end up teaching to the kids who are least prepared. And then the classes don't tend to build on one another since they are often merely modeled on the professors' narrow research interests. According to the 2010 "What

Will They Learn?" report from the American Council of Trustees and Alumni, "Colleges and universities have by and large abandoned a coherent content-rich general education curriculum, thereby allowing students to graduate with important gaps in their knowledge." Specifically, fewer than 5 percent of colleges and universities require economics. Fewer than a third require American government or history, literature, or intermediate-level foreign language. Nearly 40 percent don't require college-level mathematics.

If every crisis presents an opportunity, the opportunity here should be hard to pass up. Return colleges to their core missions, give students a more substantive education, *and* save everyone money. Who could object? The faculty, of course.

As we have already seen, most senior faculty opt out of teaching the large introductory courses and instead prefer small seminars. They can reduce even further the contact they have with students by supervising internships. As Michael Poliakoff, a researcher at the American Council for Trustees and Alumni, notes, "In many cases these internships involve very little teaching or supervision." Sometimes the faculty's lack of interest in teaching significant numbers of students reaches a laughable level. In his experience as president of Macalester College in Minnesota, Michael McPherson recalls a language professor who told him, "It is really important to teach this language—even if no students are taking it."

From the data collected by the federal government, it's very hard to discern what activities faculty are getting paid to do for what percentage of their time. As Jane Wellman notes, the standard category for reporting expenses is "instruction," but that includes all the spending for faculty, including time spent on research, serving on university committees, and so on. "If you have faculty who make sure birds don't fly in the window, they're included in that too," she jokes.

It's even harder to figure out what *tenured* professors do with their time. When Michael Poliakoff was researching an article on creating greater accountability measures in higher education, he noted that most universities wouldn't disaggregate the data on tenured and tenure-track professors. Poliakoff says, "What's hiding behind that is that senior faculty are rewarded with choosing classes they want to teach. Often students don't get the advantage of senior faculty teaching them." Whether it's in teaching or research, Poliakoff concludes that most schools have "refused responsibility to ensure that after tenure, productivity continues."

If colleges seriously wish to reduce their instructional costs, they should begin by asking professors to do more teaching. "Cutting Costs," a report by the American Council of Trustees and Alumni, asks, "In many universities, faculty teach four classes a year. In this crisis, would an increase of one class per year—which would generate a 25 percent increase in productivity—be an onerous burden?" Good question.

Why, then, do faculty generally get their way? To hear professors— even the reform-minded ones—talk, you would think it's the fault of weak-willed administrators who want nothing more than to become provost. Daniel Hamermesh, who teaches economics at the University of Texas at Austin, is fairly typical in his assessment. Tenure, he says, is not responsible for the fact that lazy or incompetent professors are allowed to stay on. With regard to a professor who wasn't showing up for his classes, Hamermesh says, "If the administrators had guts, they could get rid of him." He accuses administrators of "a lack of intestinal fortitude," though he acknowledges that the "access to court systems" by tenured professors might be making administrators think twice.

McPherson, formerly of Macalester College, says it is not a personality fault on the part of administrators. Rather, "it is usually just plain not worth it to take tenure away from an individual on grounds of incompetence. You're going to spend so much money defending that decision." McPherson, who is now president of the Spencer Foundation (which invests in educational research), says there are other "turnaround strategies" that can be used to deal with faculty who are not performing.

In fact, before we resort to such drastic measures as eliminating tenure, some professors say, why don't we institute some administrative reforms? Why don't administrators tell faculty to teach more? Why don't they use their discretion to limit the salaries of tenured professors who are not being as productive as they should be? Why don't they tell faculty members when to schedule their classes? Tenure does not technically shield faculty from having to abide by administrative orders on any of these matters.

These are good questions, and they plague every segment of higher education. But for that reason it seems unlikely that the answer is simply to be found in the craven nature of administrators. Rather, these problems are the result of structural inadequacies in the system.

Even giving administrators more tools to fight rogue faculty does not seem to have much impact. In the 1990s, in order to stave off growing public criticism of tenure, a number of universities began to implement "post-tenure review." As Anne Neal, president of the American Council of Trustees and Alumni, wrote in an article for *Academe*, "Post-tenure review was designed to keep tenure alive: it offered an accountability mechanism that would ultimately protect academic freedom." In 1996, somewhat less than a quarter of four-year colleges and universities had post-tenure review policies in place. By 1998, more than half the states had mandated some sort of post-tenure review. And by 2000, a Harvard study found that almost half of private colleges and universities had post-tenure review.

The AAUP initially opposed these policies wholeheartedly, but later altered its position. "Post-tenure review," the AAUP declared in 1999, "ought to be aimed not at accountability, but at faculty development." Much to AAUP's delight, presumably, post-tenure review has turned out to be almost wholly ineffective as a method of ensuring accountability. It has led to an infinitesimal number of actual firings. In 2002, the *Chronicle of Higher Education* reported that only one professor had been removed as a result of four years of post-tenure review in the entire Texas state system. When the University of Arizona did more than 2,700 reviews in 2001, only four professors received unsatisfactory ratings. Study after study demonstrates that few campuses have much of an idea of the goals of post-tenure review. A 1999 poll from the National Opinion Research Center found that fewer than 6 percent of faculty members strongly agree with the statement that "post-tenure review has impacted faculty performance."

The problem with post-tenure review is that it is largely under the control of the faculty themselves. In the same way that the tenure decision process suffers from an overemphasis on the importance of research over teaching, that it enforces departmental intellectual conformity, that its demands can depend entirely on "collegiality," post-tenure review simply reinforces what the tenure process has wrought. In some cases it has become an all but voluntary process; in others there are no real consequences for a negative review.

If you want to see how little power administrators—and even college presidents—have, just consider the case of Larry Summers, who was forced to resign from his position as president of Harvard because of faculty objections to his statements and policies. A few donors, including David Rockefeller, threatened to withhold almost $400 million worth of gifts to the university if Summers was pushed out. Harvard's faculty did it anyway. (This example also suggests that concerns about philanthropists having too much influence over academia—as expressed earlier by the vice president of the Ford Foundation—are not justified.)

The structural problems of college finances begin with the fact that administrators are not supposed to have ultimate financial decision-making power at the university. That is supposed to be held by the boards of trustees. Despite the efforts of groups like the American Council of Trustees and Alumni, trustees are simply not up to the task of properly overseeing universities. For most trustees, their role is very much a part-time job. They are typically busy, powerful people who have bigger fish to fry. For that matter, they are called in only when conflicts reach a boiling point. Rarely do they engage in ordinary oversight. They have largely been convinced that matters like the academic calendar, teaching loads, and curricula are matters that are best left to the experts—that is, the faculty.

On the rare occasions when administrators have the backing of the trustees, they can accomplish a good deal. Michael Crow, who was named president of Arizona State University in 2002, has completely remade the school, abolishing departments, creating new schools within the university, starting new campuses, and saving millions in administrative costs. He didn't force the faculty to go along with his plans. Rather, he offered higher salaries to the ones who did.

John Silber, the former president of Boston University, went a different route. When he came on board in 1970, he decried the deadwood on the faculty, which he referred to as "very complacent, fat and sassy." A few years later, he called professors who joined the union's campus chapter "lemmings" and "coffeehouse unionists." He fired fifteen faculty members, disbanded the football team, increased alumni donations, and hired more prestigious faculty—essentially re-creating the school. At one point, ten of the university's deans demanded his resignation, and the faculty overwhelmingly gave him a vote of no confidence. But the board of trustees stood by him.

Michael Poliakoff notes that because of that support, Silber was in a unique position. "Administrators can't solve problems much in the current situation. They are all in fear of a faculty vote of no confidence. Unless they have huge support from their boards, the faculty will run them out." Poliakoff concludes, "The board has to empower and lionize and protect the administration."

Thomas Sowell suggests one major problem: "Few, if any, people have a direct personal interest in the long-run economic or educational consequences of decisions made by officials of most colleges and universities." And to some extent, he is right. It is true, as he notes, that students are present only for a few years, and administrators often move from one university to the next. But his notion that "professors easily move from one institution to another" is generally not the case.

Faculty are in it for the long haul. They shape the university, and once they have tenure they are unlikely ever to leave. The reason why faculty don't have a "direct personal interest" in those "economic or educational consequences" is not their short term on campus but the fact that their positions are guaranteed. Tenure has skewed the incentives so that the people who should have the most concern about the economic and educational sustainability of the institution—the people who hope to be there for decades to come—actually have the least. For instance, when the economy goes south, faculty should be the ones most concerned with making sure the enrollment stays up, that consumers are still demanding the product and paying for it. "It's the opposite," notes Jane Wellman. The more students there are, the more students for faculty to teach. Why make more work for yourself?

Only when tenure is eliminated will these interests begin to change.

To make themselves more financially viable, colleges in the coming years will have to conduct some serious experiments. Mark Taylor suggests in *Crisis on Campus* that schools will have to engage in more long-distance learning and that professors will have to sell their lectures online. He believes colleges will have to form partnerships with local businesses and even with foreign governments who want to harness the power of American higher education and who have the money to pay for it.

Some schools will no doubt move in the directions that Taylor suggests. But others, meanwhile, will have to return to basics. They will have to examine what technology is important to an education and when the bells and whistles are being substituted for real learning. They will have to look at library budgets, living accommodations, and spending on food and athletics. Colleges will need to make better use of their facilities, which means that neither students nor faculty can count on three- or even four-day weekends anymore. When so much empty space is available, colleges can't continue to throw up new buildings like kids playing with blocks.

Students will need to graduate in four years (or fewer) and will need to be able to fit all of their classes in, which means they can't all be scheduled at the same time and professors can't just offer the classes they want when they want. And more than ever, students will need quality teachers. The effects of so much graduate-student and adjunct instruction of undergraduates will begin to take its toll, and parents will wonder why the senior faculty is off conducting research when Johnny still doesn't understand economics or biology or how to write a coherent paper.

If colleges want parents and students to continue to believe, in spite of the recession, that a bachelor's degree is the key to good employment prospects, professors' own narrow research interests will have to take a back seat to the need for imparting basic knowledge and skills. Core curricula of some sort will need to return. Especially in the humanities and social sciences, where there is little if any discernible value in the thousands of journal articles being written each year, professors will need to be judged on their teaching, not their publications record.

With elementary and secondary education faltering, many colleges will have to build even more significant remedial education programs. Those that don't will probably need to form partnerships with community colleges for teaching these subjects.

In general, faculty will not be pleased with these developments. They might be willing to accept a lower quality of food in the cafeteria and less spending on athletics, but other reforms will change their entire profession, and the changes will not happen without a fight.

The institution of tenure means that the fight will be weighted in favor of the faculty. The losers will be students and parents.

Colleges and universities have done their best to work around tenure. In order to save money, they have hired adjuncts. In order to reemphasize the importance of teaching, they have hired "professors of practice" who specialize in teaching and are not judged by their research. To get rid of lazy or incompetent faculty, they have offered tenured professors financial incentives to retire early. They have instituted post-tenure review policies. But ultimately none of these solutions will diminish the almost unchecked power of university faculties.

Tenure should not be eliminated for economic reasons, as Jane Wellman points out. Rather, she says, tenure is "psychologically and politically related" to the problems plaguing higher education. And that is why it should go.

It begins with the way we educate doctoral students, she says. After taking sometimes more than a decade to get a doctoral degree, young professors feel they are owed permanent job security. They have probably postponed having children and buying a house. They have been working on graduate-student stipends and part-time wages for years. "Hell yeah, they'll want the full job with benefits, including tenure," says Wellman. "But tenure is the whole reason they are being kept in this absurd position." Only once we start moving the pitcher's mound or the distance to the bases, only when we remove tenure, will it be possible to change this game.

All the problems described in this chapter will get worse before they get better. The White House has made universal access to higher education a priority. And public opinion supports the idea that we should all have a chance to go to college regardless of our ability to afford it. At the same time, thanks to the recession, states are cutting back their budgets and universities are getting less from state lawmakers. Parents and federal taxpayers will be expected to pick up the slack, but many are increasingly unwilling to hand over a blank check. They want to see how universities are adapting to tougher times. And it will take more than the Harvard faculty giving up cookies at their monthly meetings.

In order for schools to experiment with new models, to institute the real changes that need to take place, the faculty will have to get on board. Administrators—to the extent they want to—cannot make these changes happen. It's not because they are spineless bureaucrats. It's because they have no power. The boards of trustees—which are supposed to be backing the administration—are not paying attention. And the cries of parents and students will be heeded only so much. The balance of power at universities needs to be restored. The most certain way of doing that is by eliminating tenure.

# Afterword
## *The Olin Experiment*

It is not uncommon to hear people say that the United States has the best system of higher education in the world. These defenders usually follow up by explaining that American universities attract young people from countries everywhere. Given that, what are critics complaining about? Where is the crisis?

But we should be clear about why international students come to the United States. Most of them travel here to study business, engineering, computer science, math, and the physical and life sciences. America's reputation for being the place that trains top scholars comes from our elite graduate scientific research programs, not from anything else.

But what about the rest of the curriculum? And what about our own undergraduates, most of whom could never qualify for these graduate programs? In our race to get more cutting-edge scientific research out of universities, what is happening to the majority of college students who don't major in these subjects and who need a broad and strong undergraduate education?

Tenure is dragging American institutions away from their original and most important missions. Even in areas of study where one might not expect it, tenure is preventing institutions from living up to their highest potential. It is stifling the most innovative professors and preventing students from getting the education they deserve.

Eliminating tenure is a game changer for American higher education, as one college I visited aptly demonstrates.

When Richard Miller announced to his friends and colleagues that he was leaving his tenured position as dean of the University of Iowa's engineering school, he recalls, "Many of them told me I must be on dope or something." He was going to become the first president of the Franklin W. Olin College of Engineering in Massachusetts. Olin, which opened its doors ten years ago, does not offer tenure. Miller says his friends asked him, "Don't you realize that if you go there you'll never work in higher education again? They won't trust you. They'll think you turned in your union card. That you don't care about the core values of academic freedom."

Miller, a jovial man who now presides over a campus of 350 students in the suburbs of Boston, says he didn't care. Having tenure, he says, is like being placed in "golden handcuffs." "There are more important things than permanent employment. If you can't make a positive difference in the world, then why have employment?"

Franklin W. Olin was an engineer and industrialist who amassed a fortune from a variety of manufacturing enterprises in the early twentieth century. In 1938, he transferred much of his wealth to a foundation that bore his name. For the next fifty years or so, the foundation supported higher education across the country, funding buildings on more than fifty campuses. But by the 1990s, the foundation's trustees were frustrated with their inability to promote change on campus, particularly in the field of engineering. The teaching of engineering, a commission of the National Science Foundation concluded a number of years ago, had become too specialized and, unlike other disciplines, was not providing the broader education or the communication skills necessary to compete in a global business environment.

But little came of the commission's work. As Miller jokes, "One of the things they proved yet again was the historic resistance to change in higher education." And so the board of trustees of Olin decided it was time to start over. Along with a $200 million founding gift, the trustees laid out their precepts for the Olin engineering school, which included creating a "culture of innovation" and, relatedly, a decision not to offer faculty members tenure.

The culture of innovation at Olin is easily visible to any campus visitor. Unlike students in most engineering programs who spend their first three years taking physics and math before they work on designing an actual structure, Olin kids begin to design things from their first day in the classroom. I watched as one professor gave his mechanical engineering students instructions to build a bridge to span two tables. They were going to be judged on how much weight it could bear, its aesthetic appeal, and its cost efficiency. They could barely wait until they were split into groups to start sharing their ideas with one another. Miller himself describes to me a project he once worked on—building a rocket to follow Halley's Comet and collect material from it. Talking about designing a one-square-mile kite (known as a solar sail) or a giant helicopter with twelve blades, each one seven miles long, his eyes light up.

Olin students, who turn down more prestigious schools like MIT, Stanford, and Berkeley, take a variety of liberal arts courses as part of their general curriculum, and they also take courses at Babson College, a business school adjacent to their own. During their senior year, Olin kids work with a local company as "consultants" for an engineering project. Two students I spoke with were discussing a variety of concepts and products that students had worked on to help promote economic opportunity in the third world. Others have designed advanced robotic devices, worked on aeronautical design, and developed medical instruments that will result in less invasive surgeries.

When he first brought up the concept of entrepreneurship with his new faculty, Miller says, they worried that he was only talking about helping students get rich. Miller wants to help his students be successful in their careers, of course, but he seems more interested in the minting of new ideas than of new millionaires. Miller says that developing a culture of entrepreneurship has been extremely important to the school. In fact, he says, his definition of an engineer is very much like that of an entrepreneur. "Engineers are people who envision things that have never been and do whatever it takes to make them happen."

This is not an ideal that is promoted in the academy, argues Miller. And he thinks that the tenure system and peer review deserve much of the blame. "Peer review doesn't spark really creative ideas. It's a hindrance to it," he says. "Peer review makes faculty members worry about what everyone else thinks. It makes you propose only things that succeed. It makes you conservative."

The trustees at Olin have put in place some structures to prevent that kind of conservatism from taking over in the long run. In addition to the absence of tenure, the entire curriculum must be reevaluated every seven years. There are no formal departments. And students are engaged in a constant process of evaluating their education. They are asked for extensive feedback about the nature of the course and the pace of it. Alumni are surveyed six months, eighteen months, and three years after graduation to see how their Olin education has served them.

When I ask one student, Theresa Edmonds, a senior, how these policies affect her education, she says she knows her professors are taking a risk to be a part of the Olin enterprise, but she also appreciates that they are more "responsive" and that student concerns don't fall on deaf ears.

Despite the risks, the Olin vision has been appealing enough to attract an average of 140 applicants for every teaching position at Olin. While the academic job market is not very hot right now, it says something that in all but three cases Olin got their top choice to fill each slot.

Mark Somerville left a tenure-track position at Vassar to come to Olin, but he says, "It was not a hard decision to make." He says he has found that the lack of tenure has changed his teaching and research interests for the better. "When one is on the tenure track," he tells me, "the clock is ticking. There is a certain day on which you will have to produce a stack of papers. When you're making choices you're not going to ask what are some interesting directions I can go in. You'll ask what is the next step I can take that is most likely to generate more stuff so I can pass this hurdle." Not thinking about that date was "liberating," according to Somerville. And he says that what he did next became more a question of "what should we do that would advance the mission of the school?"

The passion of the Olin faculty and students to fulfill the school's mission is unmistakable. Miller calls them "a community of zealots." Not exactly what you'd expect from a bunch of engineers, perhaps. But then, giving up tenure may do some strange things to people.

# Suggested Readings

Philip G. Altback, Patricia J. Gumport, and D. Bruce Johnstone, eds., *In Defense of American Higher Education* (Baltimore: Johns Hopkins University Press, 2001).

Ryan C. Amacher and Roger E. Meiners, *Faulty Towers: Tenure and the Structure of Higher Education* (Oakland, Calif.: Independent Institute, 2004).

Martin Anderson, *Impostors in the Temple: American Intellectuals Are Destroying Our Universities and Cheating Our Students of Their Future* (New York: Simon and Schuster, 1992).

Gordon B. Arnold, *The Politics of Faculty Unionization: The Experience of Three New England Universities* (Westport, Conn.: Bergin and Garvey, 2000).

Roger G. Baldwin and Jay L. Chronister, *Teaching Without Tenure: Policies and Practices for a New Era* (Baltimore: Johns Hopkins University Press, 2001).

Jacques Barzun, *The American University: How It Runs, Where It Is Going* (New York: Harper and Row, 1968).

William G. Bowen and Julie Ann Sosa, *Prospects for Faculty in the Arts and Sciences* (Princeton, N.J.: Princeton University Press, 1989).

Richard P. Chait, ed., *The Questions of Tenure* (Cambridge, Mass.: Harvard University Press, 2002).

John G. Cross and Edie N. Goldenberg, *Off-Track Profs: Nontenured Teachers in Higher Education* (Cambridge, Mass.: MIT Press, 2009).

Matthew W. Finkin and Robert C. Post, *For the Common Good: Principles of Academic Freedom* (New Haven, Conn.: Yale University Press, 2009).

Stanley Fish, *Save the World on Your Own Time* (Oxford: Oxford University Press, 2008).

Amy Gajda, *The Trials of Academe: The New Era of Campus Litigation* (Cambridge, Mass.: Harvard University Press, 2009).

Evan Gerstmann and Matthew J. Streb, eds., *Academic Freedom at the Dawn of a New Century: How Terrorism, Governments and Culture Wars Impact Free Speech* (Stanford, Calif.: Stanford University Press, 2006).

Andrew Hacker and Claudia Dreifus, *Higher Education? How Colleges Are Wasting Our Money and Failing Our Kids—and What We Can Do About It* (New York: Times Books, 2010).

Donald E. Heller and Madeleine B. d'Ambrosio, eds., *Generational Shockwaves and the Implications for Higher Education* (Cheltenham, UK: Edward Elgar, 2008).

David Horowitz, *The Professors: The 101 Most Dangerous Academics in America* (Washington, D.C.: Regnery, 2001).

Philo A. Hutcheson, *A Professional Professoriate: Unionization, Bureaucratization and the AAUP* (Nashville, Tenn.: Vanderbilt University Press, 2000).

Christopher Jencks and David Riesman, *The Academic Revolution* (Garden City, N.Y.: Doubleday, 1968).

Roger Kimball, *Tenured Radicals: How Politics Has Corrupted Our Higher Education* (New York: HarperCollins, 1990).

David L. Kirp, *Shakespeare, Einstein, and the Bottom Line* (Cambridge, Mass.: Harvard University Press, 2003).

James M. Lang, *Life on the Tenure Track: Lessons from the First Year* (Baltimore: Johns Hopkins University Press, 2005).

Cary Nelson, *No University Is an Island* (New York: New York University Press, 2010).

William L. O'Neill, *A Bubble in Time: America During the Interwar Years, 1989–2001* (Chicago: Ivan R. Dee, 2009).

David D. Perlmutter, *Promotion and Tenure Confidential* (Cambridge, Mass.: Harvard University Press, 2010).

Ellen Schrecker, *The Lost Soul of Higher Education: Corporatization, the Assault on Academic Freedom and the End of the American University* (New York: New Press, 2010).

Bruce L. R. Smith, Jeremy D. Mayer, and A. Lee Fritschler, eds., *Closed Minds? Politics and Ideology in American Universities* (Washington, D.C.: Brookings Institution, 2008).

Thomas Sowell, *Economic Facts and Fallacies* (New York: Basic Books, 2008).

Charles J. Sykes, *ProfScam: Professors and the Demise of Higher Education* (Washington, D.C.: Regnery, 1988).

Mark C. Taylor, *Crisis on Campus: A Bold Plan for Reforming Our Colleges and Universities* (New York: Alfred A Knopf, 2010).

Cathy A. Trower, ed., *Policies on Faculty Appointment: Standard Practices and Unusual Arrangements* (Bolton, Mass.: Anker Publishing, 2000).

Jennifer Washburn, *University Inc.: The Corporate Corruption of Higher Education* (New York: Basic Books, 2005).

Burton A. Weisbrod, Jeffrey P. Ballou, and Evelyn D. Asch, *Mission and Money: Understanding the University* (Cambridge: Cambridge University Press, 2008).

# Index

AAUP. *See* American Association of University Professors

academic freedom, 17; AAUP for, 25–26, 33; accountability and, 19, 37; autonomy compared to, 26–27; common sense about, 30; conflict and, 22–23; corporations related to, 34–36; courts and, 28–29; dialogues on, 18–19; donors and, 18; faculty on, 19–20; finances and, 36–37; FIRE for, 131; First Amendment and, 27–28; gender studies and, 40; for Holocaust denial, 33–34; irrelevance of, 20–21, 20n1, 31–33, 41; legal definition of, 27–28; meaning of, 26; at private universities, 27; at public universities, 27–28, 27n2; during recession, 18; religious institutions and, 21; technology and, 19; tenure and, 19–20, 29–30; termination and, 23; transparency and, 19; university politics related to, 38–41; vocational courses and, 31–34; war and, 18

*Academic Questions*, 6

*The Academic Revolution* (Jencks and Riesman), 11, 49

accountability: academic freedom and, 19, 37; of faculty, 161; in job market, 127; research universities without, 23–24, 25; of tenure faculty, 161–62

ACTA. *See* American Council of Trustees and Alumni

adjunct faculty, 10; AFT and, 88–89, 104–5; competition among, 79–80; continuous employment status for, 104; doctoral degrees and, 92; education quality and, 85–87, 93; grade inflation by, 88; higher education financial problems and, 152–53; increase in, 77–78;

sciences, 55, 172; publishing in,
58–59; research universities and,
24; unions and, 112; university
politics and, 122
Shapiro, Carl, 119
Silber, John, 7–8, 65, 109–10, 165
Simpson, John, 114
Smith, Bruce, 22, 121–22
Smith, Dee Montgomery, 115
Smith, Philip, 113–14
Sokal, Alan, 54
*A Soldier's Heart* (Samet), 140–41
Somerville, Mark, 174–75
Somin, Ilya, 124–25
Sowell, Thomas, 146–47, 154, 160,
165
Sparks, John, 137
Stanford, Mrs. Leland, 23
Stanford University, 23, 25
State University of New York
(SUNY), 113–14
Stern, Charlotta, 122–23, 126–27
Stimson, Catherine R., 80
students, xi–xii, 155; corporations
with, 36; graduate students as,
109–10; international students,
171; for job market, 67, 148; post-
graduate salaries of, 148; problems
of, 75; teaching evaluation by, 66–
67; undergraduate graduation rate
of, 85–86; undergraduate return
rate of, 86. *See also* graduate
students
Summers, Larry, 164
SUNY. *See* State University of New
York

Supreme Court: faculty and, 27–29,
105–7; on First Amendment,
27–28; *Garcetti v. Ceballos*, 27–29;
*NLRB v. Yeshiva University*, 105–
7; tenure and, 105–6
Surber, Jere, 123

Taylor, Mark, 5, 64–65, 149, 166
teaching: academic schedule for,
160; administrators and, 11, 160;
Cherry Teaching Award, 45–49,
64, 69; faculty's choices for,
160–62; professors of practice for,
62; progressiveness and, 56–57;
publishing compared to, 8, 9, 111,
167; salaries for, 49; technology
in, 157–58; tenure and, 50–63,
65, 160
teaching compared to research, 9–10;
adjunct faculty and, 90; classics in,
57–58; contracts for, 51; finances
and, 51, 55; in humanities, 59–61;
mutual reinforcement of, 53–56;
public opinion on, 52, 55, 148;
specialization and, 59–61; tenure
and, 50, 62–63; time and, 49–51,
56
teaching evaluation, 8–9; by
administrators, 65–66; Cherry
Awards as, 45–49, 64, 69; between
institutions, 63–64; job market
related to, 67; measurement in,
64–65, 66–68; *New York Times*
on, 66; on outcomes, 68; by
peers, 65; research and, 61–69;
school rankings and, 67–69;

# About the Author

**Naomi Schaefer Riley** is a former *Wall Street Journal* editor and writer whose work focuses on higher education, religion, philanthropy, and culture. She is the author of *God on the Quad: How Religious Colleges and the Missionary Generation Are Changing America* (2005). Ms. Riley's writings have appeared in the *Wall Street Journal*, the *New York Times*, the *Washington Post*, the *Boston Globe*, the *LA Times*, and the *Chronicle of Higher Education*, among other publications. She graduated magna cum laude from Harvard University with a degree in English and government. She lives in the suburbs of New York with her husband, Jason, and their two children.